First Buy a Field

The Realists Guide to Self-Sufficiency

By Rosamund Young

Published by The Good Life Press Ltd 2008

Copyright © Rosamund Young

ISBN 978 1 90487 130 9
A catalogue record for this book is available from the British Library.

Published by
The Good Life Press Ltd
PO Box 536
Preston
PR2 9ZY

www.goodlifepress.co.uk

Set by The Good Life Press Ltd.
Illustrations by Rebecca Peacock
Printed and bound in Great Britain
by Cromwell Press.

First Buy a Field

The Realists Guide to Self-Sufficiency

By Rosamund Young

Chapters

The Preamble

Before you can make your first recipe using your own home grown ingredients you will need to buy a field. Try to find one with a stream of pure water running through or round the edge of it and one which has never been sprayed with chemicals, has power lines neither overhead nor underground and is not about to be traversed by pipelines. So far, so easy. Take note of the different types of lichen - they are sure indicators of pure air.

Plant lots of trees: willow and alder near the stream and oak, ash and all sorts of fruit trees. While you are waiting for the trees to grow so that you can cut some down to build yourself a house and have fuel to fire the wood-burning stove, buy a cow, three sheep, two pigs and, of course, some hens.

While you are waiting for the cow to calve, the sheep to lamb, the pigs to farrow and the hens to start laying, plant a patch of wheat, scouring, if necessary, the whole of Europe to find a nice, old variety which has never seen the inside of a laboratory or been considered as a suitable prospect for the next round of genetic modification. Then cultivate a vegetable and soft fruit garden.

While you are waiting for the wheat and the rest of your crops to ripen, construct a small watermill to grind the corn. Plunder the local library or get to know your field-owning neighbours and learn from them the traditional secrets of making butter and cheese, keeping in mind the last two pearls of wisdom from the ancient (Chinese?) proverb "...if you want to be happy for a week, kill a pig and if you want to be happy for a lifetime, take up gardening."

Should you wish to experience this week of happiness, you could buy various books, videos or DVDs which will explain in detail how to kill a pig and you are almost home and dry.

By the time you are ready to move into your new home and the stove is heating up nicely, the butter is made, the flour milled and the eggs from the 50th generation of hens assembled on your handmade table, the rheumatism in your hands may be the one factor threatening to prevent you from actually beating the cake mixture yourself. You could then summon one of your great grand-daughters, who you had thoughtfully advised to buy her own field with a ready made house, established herds and flocks, a wind powered cold store and freezers, so that her first self-sufficient cake was achieved while still in her twenties. She could then beat it for you.

You had decided long ago, at the age of eleven to be exact, following your second cookery lesson at school, (the first having demonstrated how to bake an apple) that your first self-sufficient recipe with home grown ingredients would be what your cookery mistress called Welsh Cheese Cakes, although she never satisfactorily explained why as they contained no cheese.

So you watch as your great granddaughter rolls out the pastry, which you did manage to make the night before, so that the excessive-seeming amount of liquid could be absorbed in a leisurely way by the home-milled wholemeal flour. She rolls it to your instructions very thinly, lines a tray of twelve small tins and carefully places a spoonful of jam made from yellow Pershore Egg Plums (which merit a chapter to themselves) in each. If you decided to grow and refine your own sugar beet, she can then beat the sugar (otherwise honey and butter), add the eggs and flour and you can then bake your first truly self-sufficient recipe at the age of nearly 89.

During the lifetime it has taken you to realise that if you chose the life you thought would be healthy it would very nearly kill you, you will have learnt quite a lot of interesting things such as how to milk a cow and use the dairy produce, how to kill a pig and keep yourself fully occupied (a Chinese euphemism for happy) for a week and myriad other agricultural skills. You will also have learnt the importance of having pure water, not just for your own sake but for that of your animals too; a milking cow might drink up to 10 to 15 gallons of water each day and any fluoride or aluminium will certainly be a pollutant in the milk she gives. You might even have begun to understand how all the characters in the natural world seem to interact and how they all instinctively know their own parts by heart, unlike we humans who must be taught but forever make mistakes and cause no end of problems.

You will undoubtedly have struggled with your chosen life, learning (though all too slowly) all the time but never really able to benefit from your newfound knowledge. You told your children and their children how to avoid the mistakes you had made but you forgot, as we humans invariably do, that they are human too and insisted on the right to make their own mistakes, thus ensuring that the most vulnerable and most powerful species carried on proliferating and destroying its own environment. But all the time you remained cheerful in the firm belief that you were at least doing your very best.

Rosamund Young
Kites Nest Farm

1.
My House Cow

You and your husband have been slaving away at university for years, collecting degrees, doctorates and many books on organic farming, alternative medicine, self-sufficiency, wind and water power, weaving, spinning, hurdle-making, walling and wholefood cookery. You are now longing to put it all into practice.

You must now find a field.

Your ideology runs up against practical, financial limitations. You do not want to use your hard won academic achievements to earn money in a conventional, competitive workplace and yet you both want the perfect field to start your future perfect lifestyle. One of your tutors remarks, perhaps rather too tartly, that the only honest way to be self-sufficient is to be born into abject poverty and then to have to survive or perish. You try for the rest of your life to forget or deny this but fail.

As a practical compromise you both decide to work, but spend every spare minute looking for just the right field, which you eventually find and then set about making 'a go' of it. You plant trees and cultivate a garden, planting each vegetable next to a nice, friendly companion plant. You also measure the current in the stream to see if it will be able to turn a mill wheel and begin the arduous process of gaining permission to build a house.

Your House Cow

You remember reading about choosing a house cow: 'It is not so much the breed of cow you need to decide on, but the nature of the individual. Different breeds do have different characteristics and those are important, but the breed is not in itself the deciding factor, nor for that matter are the niceties of conformation. Instinct should take precedence over a tally of attributes; it's not like an arranged marriage, it's to do with love and all that that entails. You need a cow who looks at you squarely and without fear. She needs a long, clean tail and a loose, wobbly dewlap. Cows reared in stressful commercial herds often have tight, small dewlaps. There is no finer or complete food than milk but it must come from a contented cow grazing natural, species rich pasture and drinking pure water. The milk must never be pasteurised: this heating process destroys everything worth having in milk. It is perfectly possible to live on milk alone for a considerable time (certainly for up to two years); it is doubtful if there is another substance so uniquely sustaining.

Unless you milk your own cow or at least buy milk from a cow known personally by you and milked by someone you trust, you would be better off not having milk at all. But there is a catch to making the decision to abstain from buying milk; you will have to go without butter, cream, yoghurt, most types of chocolate, most biscuits, many cakes and quite a few puddings."

You decide to buy a cow.

None of the organic farmers you approach will sell one. They all love them too much.

While at university you and your husband spent your holidays visiting all sorts of agricultural enterprises from remote crofts to high-tech farms, gathering as much knowledge as possible and you made a point of tasting the milk from many different breeds of cow, always inquiring minutely into their diet. It was not possible to be certain but it seemed to you that the type of forage they ate determined the flavour of the milk. The science fascinated you both. You learnt that the fat globules in milk from Ayrshire cows, for instance, were more evenly distributed than in many breeds, making it easier to digest and therefore more suitable for babies and the infirm. You also found that Jersey cows produce milk which is altogether too rich for your palate and Friesian milk, once the cream has been skimmed off to make butter, is too much like water. Your husband even unearthed an article describing the life of a talented chemist, Geoffrey Austin Young, who began making discoveries about the chemistry of milk as far back as 1911.

He discovered that when milk is pasteurised the molecular structure is altered, with the result that the Calcium Phosphate becomes insoluble in blood yet it is the Calcium Phosphate that is essential in the human body for the growth and health of both the bones and teeth. He prophesied that, if pasteurised milk ever became popular, the nation would suffer from bad teeth, brittle bones and bone related illnesses.

The article went on to describe how in 1972 one of his sons, John, developed prostate cancer and followed the strict diet advocated by his father for curing cancer, refraining from eating any foods containing white sugar or salt, eating fresh fruit and vegetables and, most importantly, drinking one pint of unpasteurised organic milk a day, plus at least one, but preferably several, teaspoons of black treacle. He cured the cancer and it did not recur.

You come across various references to conjugated linoleic acid or CLA which, you read, is present in organically produced milk and bears some close connection to white clover. You then go immediately to inspect the species in your field and identify eleven in the first square yard, including white clover; no wonder your milk tastes so good.

There are no Ayrshires to be found within a hundred miles and, as you do not want to make your cow travel too far, you settle for a Welsh Black with horns from a conventional herd and immediately embark on her conversion. Your mother, who you keep closely informed of your progress, wonders if this would resemble converting from Anglicanism to Catholicism; you tell her you will try to explain when you have waded through The Soil Association's regulations.

To your dismay you discover that this lovely bovine will never actually achieve organic status herself, no matter how hard she or you might try. However, her offspring will. The years pass and you sow and hoe and reap and thresh and grind and bake. Calves come and go both literally and figuratively and, by the time your cow's first daughter is three, you get your first glass of home-produced organic milk and can embark on a variety of milk-based recipes.

Over the next seven decades you get to know quite a few cows and discover that they are all individuals with vastly different temperaments. You find it is perfectly possible to gain the trust of an unfriendly cow because she will only be unfriendly for a very good reason. It is also possible to betray the trust of a friendly cow by unsympathetic behaviour. You know by instinct that if a cow takes an instant dislike to someone, it is almost certainly his or her fault. In the short term you can deceive a cow once and make her do something she might not instinctively want to, but in the longer term you find that you cannot use the same trick a second time; cows are clever and do things willingly if what they are being asked to do is reasonable.

You establish, beyond doubt, that the milk from a sweet natured, easy-going cow will not only taste better but will do you more good. All the human mothers you talk to say they know for certain that when they are breast-feeding, the baby is immediately affected by changes in the milk quality, most of which relate to their own mood, health, stress level, psychological well-being and general state of happiness. It comes as no surprise to them when you share your new discovery about cows' milk. You begin to feel that you will never be the first person to discover anything. Perhaps this is how all writers feel with regard to Shakespeare; no matter what they might think of, he invariably said it first.

You both like porridge so planting a patch of oats seems a logical thing to do. This plan is beset with problems from the start. The first farmer to offer advice asks you if you know how to de-groat an oat which leaves you both silent. He tries to explain a bit about the process of making oats edible but you stop concentrating half way through his meandering explanation and find yourself day dreaming. You are now beginning to think about buying a box of porridge oats instead to tide you over and you only refocus on your farming guru as he says the words 'naked oats.' You ask him to repeat them and your spirits revive somewhat as he tells you that these interesting seeds do not require an elaborate preparation. Your optimism is, however, short-lived as he begins to question the suitability of your land for growing oats of any kind.

Unfortunately this is just the start of a disturbing number of compromises you reluctantly agree to make over the next few years. You do eventually manage to find some naked oat seed but the weather and the aspect of the field both conspire against a fruitful crop; purchased porridge oats in a cardboard box becomes a permanent feature, but at least you know that it is made using your own milk.

Accidental Cheese Making

You have already learnt how to make yoghurt and several different types of cheese (well, in theory,

anyway) from books and you are delighted to find that putting it into practice produces delicious results, greatly expanding your repertoire of recipes. You both enjoy this activity and sometimes work together and sometimes individually. However you both agree that one of the many privileges of having a field and consuming all the produce yourselves is that you do not have to obey the rules which govern products destined for retail. From time to time you can even allow some milk to make itself into 'accidental cheese.'

In winter you put a stainless steel container of milk in the airing cupboard for three days before straining it through a muslin cloth, after which you sometimes lightly press it to remove excess whey.

In a warm summer, you can leave the milk almost anywhere and it becomes cheese quite quickly. You occasionally make an 'accidental yoghurt' too, in line with your resistance to overheating or pasteurising milk.

You find that by warming the milk to a mere 110°F and adding a teaspoon of plain yoghurt (or alternatively by adding nothing) you create an edible substance. The only obstacle to success is the absence of volunteers to consume it.

You must now come to terms with the inevitable seasonal fluctuations in the quantity and quality of your milk. You may have perfected the art of making and storing hard cheese but keeping butter to tide you over the lean times proves far more of a challenge. You learn many things every day and despair a bit most days.

2.
A Way with Wheat

Your nearest neighbour is a retired farmer in his nineties. He tells you that he kept a hundredweight of wheat, a handful of which he germinated each year. In the thirtieth year of his experiment none of the grains of wheat would germinate. This fascinates you and you try, and succeed, in not mentioning a fact you seem to remember learning at school about the wheat carefully stored in airtight jars in Tutankhamun's tomb still being viable 2000 years later.

The patch of wheat you have planted is quite small so you are confident that once it is fully ripened you will be able to cut it with whatever implements you have available: scythe, shears or even a pair of scissors. You bind the stems and hang the wheat upside down from a beam in a cool, airy place and hope that the wheat berries will drop out on to the floor. They do not. After a time you place bundles of wheat in clean, untreated paper sacks, tying the tops and hanging them so that any wheat is collected in the sacks. Almost none falls out. Wheat, you decide, is notoriously stubborn so you set about devising your own method of small-scale threshing.

You start by spreading out the mini sheaves on clean sheets on the lawn on a warm, dry day. You then beat or thresh them with tightly bound bundles of willow twigs. The threshed corn is then gently poured from a height, back onto another clean sheet in front of a household fan which blows off the lightest chaff. You then sort the wheat by hand to remove any unwanted weed seeds, which you feed to the hens. All the time, though, you find yourself wondering whether you should have bought or borrowed a combine harvester which would have done the job in minutes.

Your research and enquiries reveal that millers and bakers famously and interestingly disagree about whether to keep the wheat for several months, or even years, before milling it into flour, or using it straight away. You accept several invitations to taste the products from various bakers before deciding you prefer to keep it for a minimum of three months.

Whilst performing this Herculean labour you find yourself becoming quite hungry and buy a few pounds of flour from the nearest organic stockist.

It soon becomes clear that it will take years before you have enough wheat for all your baking needs and to feed the hens, as from each harvest some seed must be saved for planting. You then decide to buy a very large sack of flour but a few months later you wish you had not done so because if flour, however alluringly cheap it may be in bulk, is not used within a certain time it deteriorates. The oil in the wheatgerm is released when it is crushed and not only will some of the goodness evaporate but, like any other oil, it will eventually become rancid. One of the old, wise country dwellers you have been so sweetly interrogating bluntly points out that you are spending too much time learning (a euphemism for enjoying yourself) and not enough time doing, which is why the flour was not being used as quickly as it should have been. You walk home deep in thought but the next morning you actually make some bread.

Making Bread

The first loaves you make with your own wheat and your own water are absolutely perfect. Even the salt you use comes with a meticulous pedigree, having been deposited over centuries in Cheshire when it was still part of the sea and the yeast comes from a manufacturer who swears he has never and would never use any new-fangled techniques. This cheers you up enormously. You get up extra early the next day and set about making several batches for friends and relations. All sixteen loaves are either as heavy as bricks or under-cooked and tasteless. You feel despondent. Over the succeeding twenty-seven years you work so hard to acquire this skill, developing a sixth, or even a seventh sense, and in the end you know by instinct when your mood, the relative humidity, the wind speed, the oven temperature, the amount of kneading, the moisture content and the exact blend of wheat varieties are right and finally you secretly know yourself to be a master baker.

The first crop of wheat you plant in the spring is a variety called Timmo. Finding enough seed is hugely difficult but in the end you buy 2lbs and begin the process of increasing your seed stock. A few seasons later you find someone willing to sell some Flanders wheat and this you plant in the autumn. Each crop has its specific attributes depending on the prevailing conditions. Flanders grains are large, golden and plump. Timmo grains are small, hard and dull. Neither variety makes superb bread on its own, so you slowly become a blender as well as a miller of wheat.

As you get older your store of wheat from different years increases and you find that the best bread is often composed with a percentage of wheat from four or five harvests. You also notice that the colour and plumpness varies according to the soil and the amount of sunshine. Some years later you acquire a map sporting many colours denoting soil types. You are excited to be able to pinpoint various mini swathes of distinctive composition within your own field's boundaries.

Repeatedly you are warned that it is not possible to make bread from English wheat but you prove everyone wrong and thereafter 'everyone' comes to see you often, wishing to eat your bread regularly, just to make sure. Using the whole grain seems so unavoidably sensible you cannot understand how anyone would want to use an impoverished grade of flour. A huge percentage of the nutritionally beneficial components is forfeited as soon as any extraction occurs. You use 100 percent home-grown flour in everything you make from bread, pastry, biscuits and cakes to sauces. But you never stop worrying about the yeast.

Every few months you experiment with sourdough. You lament having to use so unsuitable a name, which is far from self-explanatory. To begin with you follow written advice and carefully note down everything you do with the firm intention of eventually making a decision about which method produces the best results and following it thereafter. Sixty-three years later you come across your notes, marvel briefly at their neatness and detail and then burn them with a wry smile. Time is one thing you are never going to have enough of and the bread evolves interestingly once you stop reading, and start feeling what to do.

Making Sourdough

Your first attempt to make sourdough uses a tiny amount of flour mixed with an equally tiny amount of water which you knead and leave in a warm, draft free place. Twenty-four hours later you 'feed' it with more flour and water and repeat the kneading process. The more you do this the more it begins to feel like keeping a pet. It grows. You feed it and it grows a bit more. After a week you have a reasonable sized piece of dough and risk making your first sourdough bread using this 'pet' as the starter culture, in place of yeast.

All goes according to plan, although the slightly vinegary taste takes a little getting used to but then, a few weeks later, disaster strikes and, in your habitual hurry, you forget to save a small piece for the next batch and cook it all. A friend remarks that you have 'cooked your mother.' It seems that she has, unknown to you, been making sourdough successfully for years, and in the middle of London, of all places. She calls her starter the 'mother culture.' You are not, after all, the pioneer you thought you were.

As you are really serious about self-sufficiency you try making some more sourdough bread with a starter using plums, picked early in the day with a bloom of wild yeast on them. You wash a couple in a drop of warm water and use this liquid to make the dough. After multiple attempts and multiple failures you finally feel an affinity with this dough; it seems more alive and you risk baking a loaf after only four days. It looks superb and tastes real; the loaf is light but the slices are substantial and filling. Not everyone likes it but you grow to value its distinctive qualities and at least you have the satisfaction of knowing the yeast has not been genetically modified. You keep a small piece in a jam jar in the fridge until you need it. The plum starter is delicious to begin with but it gets stronger each time you make a batch of bread. You feel resistant to the idea of buying a culture; you feel you can surely be self-sufficient in wild yeast.

In the end, after many interesting experiments, and voluminous reading to try to understand the science of sourdough bread, you dispense with plums and use flour and water: 2 ounces of flour plus 2 ounces of water mixed and kneaded and left for a day in a warm place. You add the same quantities again twenty-four hours later and on the third day you add 2 ounces of flour with 1 ounce of water. On the fourth day you add a further 6 ounces of flour and 4 ounces of water. On the fifth day you take 8 ounces of this starter and mix it with 10 ounces of flour and 6 ounces of water. You leave this in the warm until is has expanded for about 4 hours. The remainder of the starter you put in a clean glass jar in the fridge until next time.

Although you consult many and varied people and books you always have what seems like far too much starter to store. You are tempted on occasions to start baking bread on a commercial scale as the wild yeast dough seems to increase faster than you can eat it. A different recipe you will read at some time in the future admits there may be some of the main ingredient left over (in this case it is potatoes) and it suggests you 'do something else with them'. You have long been exercised by this prospect in relation to wild yeast.

In the next stage of this wild yeast bread saga you mix, in a separate bowl, 1 pound of flour, an eighth of an ounce of salt and 12 ounces of water. You knead this for about 10 minutes until it is soft and smooth. You then add the starter which has had its four-hour 'active rest' and knead again. You leave this in a damp bowl covered with an inflated plastic bag for an hour. This is then carefully lifted, pulled and stretched, though you did not realise this was what you were doing until some forty or so years later when suddenly all the questions you had agonised over were answered when a fine friend lent you the definitive book on bread making. The dough is then dipped in flour to coat it all over and left to rise in a proving basket for a few hours (3-5) in a warm place. When you gently press it and the indentation is slow to recover, it is time to cook it. You tip the dough gently onto a baking tray lined with parchment, slash it deftly thrice and cook it at 220°C for 10 minutes and then reduce the heat to 200° for a further half an hour. You learn by trial and error when any loaf is ready, always remembering that it is far better to be slightly overcooked than underdone.

Initially this seems like a long, slow, time-consuming procedure but you discover some fascinating facts: the natural yeasts combine with enzymes enhancing bacteria which digest the starch and change the pH level and this makes the bread more digestible. During the slow process of fermentation the nutritional properties of the dough change; the carbohydrate content is lowered and the availability of minerals increases. The more often you make wild yeast bread, the easier it becomes. You simply learn instinctively that the quantities used are approximate as your flour will vary from harvest to harvest. You then pause to wonder one day if flour from a shop always has precisely the same moisture content.

When you were young you always followed recipes to the letter. You still do if they cannot be improved upon. Most of the alterations and variations you risk are dictated by time, or the lack of it. The luxury of doing something properly usually has to be forgone; everything has to be fitted in, so that no essential activity suffers. When making wild yeast bread you have to accept the whole, slow concept and that does not leave many corners to cut. However, kneading dough continually for ten minutes seems like a very long time as exercising for five minutes can seem like an eternity, although when working outside for four hours the time flies by. Sometimes the dough only receives a four-minute-knead.

However, you still make bread with yeast too. From the first day you calculate that you have enough home-grown wheat to make you able to be self-sufficient in bread, you vow not to buy any more. You buy a mill and jump headlong into your self-imposed commitment. One day though, one of those days when everything has gone wrong, you are wearily climbing the stairs to go to bed when you suddenly remember there is no bread for breakfast. In those, now far off days bread was your staple, and a day without bread was unthinkable. Your initial reaction is horror but that soon gives way to laughter. No one forced you to buy a field. You go back down to the kitchen and put some more wood on the fire. You never forget again.

Buying a mill is going to be exciting. You make endless enquiries and time after time you are told about a French, table-sized mill with proper stones for grinding, but everyone agrees that it is too slow. Nonetheless, the sound of it appeals to you. Three people offer to lend you one but they all forget, repeatedly. All sorts of trails leading you to second-hand mills for sale go cold and then, one day, your husband buys one from a local agricultural merchant. It has been designed to be used with a variety of sieves for milling food for calves, pigs and hens. It is a bit ugly and cumbersome and, as the supply of spare parts has dried up, it is being offered at a bargain price. You both agree it will do for the meantime.

The first thirty-six years of 'the meantime' just fly by while you are meaning to find a better one. It works perfectly, never needs any maintenance and before long it is considered to be your most useful and valuable possession. You now concede that your little stream will only ever have the power to turn a mill wheel during flash flooding once every second decade.

The capacity of the mill's hopper is about 30lbs but you never grind more than 9 at one go and often only 2 or 3. You have learnt to riddle wheat and the swinging, swirling motion is now part of your being. It is a primeval feeling. Quite possibly you are the first and only person ever to have used such a lengthy and eccentric method of preparing wheat for grinding but it feels somehow ancient and important. You find that by holding the riddle horizontal to your body and swirling it in a circular motion, gathering speed with each of four or five successive revolutions and then stopping with a slight backward jerk/swirl, much of the lighter chaff rises to the top and accumulates conveniently. You soon become adept at recognising weed seeds and decide that many are probably safe to be cooked anyway.

You take care not to pour any wheat berries onto the air intake as you feed the hopper, and you watch over it as it grinds, noisily, and push the last few ounces down the chutes by hand to prevent it running dry and overheating. The slightly warm, golden flour is ready to use immediately for bread but you always make sure it is cold before making pastry.

In the beginning, which time span lasts seventeen years, you make all the bread by hand, wearing your knuckles out in the process. The gift of a very old, large, dough-mixer transforms bread making days and you never cease to be grateful to the man who designed the dough hook.

You put 2lbs 3 ounces of freshly milled, and therefore slightly warm, wholemeal flour and half an ounce of salt into a bowl. You then sprinkle 4 teaspoons of dried yeast into a cup of warm water containing a teaspoon of sugar. Your field is in such a remote location that it is impractical and expensive to buy fresh yeast; dried yeast is therefore a permanent item on your never-to-be-non-existent shopping list. As soon as this mixture forms a frothy head and looks as if it is climbing out of the cup, you tip it into an indentation in the flour and you then add just the right amount of warm water to form a perfect dough (1lb 6 ounces). When the flour is new, by which you mean when the wheat is only six months to two years old, the required amount of water will be roughly a quarter of a pint less than you will need five years later when the wheat will have dried out. It is all down to feel. The dough must almost stick to your hands. In fact, if it does actually stick, although slightly inconvenient, it is far better than being too dry. Initially you use one pound of warm water in addition to the yeast mixture. Five years later you need one pound six ounces. It all depends on where you keep the wheat.

When you are using the large mixer with a 9lb load of flour, 2-2.25 ounces of salt, 8 teaspoons of yeast (the quantity needed seems to decrease disproportionately to the increase in flour) and as the dough hook kneads on its slowest speed, you gently add warm water until the dough looks right. You stop the machine, feel the dough and make the appropriate adjustments.

Whatever quantity of flour you use it usually takes about an hour to rise: slightly less on a hot day and slightly more on a cold one. The dough is kneaded for a second time, divided and placed in tins (roughly 1lb 12 ounces- 2lbs per tin) When you only use 2lbs of flour you cook 4 bap-shaped loaves of roughly 14 ounces each. Sometimes you use a slow rising method with a tiny quantity of yeast, leaving the dough to rise in a cold place for 8 hours before the second kneading.

You always cook bread in a pre-heated, very hot oven and allow the heat to fall gently during cooking. The baps take half an hour and the tins three quarters of an hour; you turn the loaves in tins upside down after half an hour and return them to the oven for the remaining quarter of an hour. You always tap cooked bread with your knuckle to make sure it sounds hollow and then you know for sure that it is cooked.

3.
Hens

You now have some wheat and weed seeds to supplement your hens' diet. Your hens are not only beautiful but clever. This surprises your husband. You tell him it should not: hens are birds, birds are clever and hens are very clever. You both admit that they make far better companions than most so-called pets. You look after the hens and they look after you.

When the weather is fine they keep themselves intensely occupied investigating everything that does and does not move in the garden and orchard. They develop a routine which, although it incorporates daily variations, always ends with an early evening stroll along the hard road in front of the house. Whenever it rains they tend to loiter near the house and run to meet you every time you open the door. Sometimes they sit on the doormat, forcing you to step over them. They remind you of the way children behave when they cannot go outside to play. As you are always busy you always try to ignore them and you always fail, clearing a place for them inside a pen, shed or stable where they can dust bathe and sing.

All your friends at school remember exactly where they were and what they were doing at the precise moment they heard that President Kennedy had been assassinated. You do not. But you do remember where you were and what you were doing the day Edwina Currie admitted that there was salmonella in most egg production in this country. You already suspected this but it re-enforced your determination to buy a field, buy some hens and never buy an egg again. In this you succeed.

You have read just about every word that has ever been written about keeping hens but during the years you keep learning new things. You try, for a short time, keeping more hens than you need and selling the surplus eggs. Sadly, like every other venture you attempt for making money, this fails. This is partly because the very nice people who come to buy your eggs stay and talk for too long, forget to bring any money and when they eventually come back to pay, stay too long all over again or they forget to bring their egg boxes back. This egg box charade was dreamed up to circumnavigate the rules which seemed likely to be introduced on testing small flocks for salmonella which would have made it effectively illegal to sell eggs from an untested flock and

too expensive for a small flock owner to test. If you
sell empty boxes (or lease them) and give away the
eggs inside, you can trade. In the event, fortunately,
small flocks were exempted if they fulfilled certain
conditions.

So, for the rest of time, you only keep a few hens. To
begin with you feel a bit lost but soon learn to cope
during the time they stop laying: when there are eggs you
use them, when there are none, you eat something else.
This is what you love about owning a field and never
going near a supermarket. You eat what is in season and
enjoy the wonderful things more for having to anticipate
and wait for them. However, all your animals teach you
something most days and you discover that by learning
to understand your hens they reward you. If you give
them an interesting and wide variety of things to eat and
fresh milk as well as abundant water to drink they will
lay more eggs per year.

You have to make a decision about whether to breed your
own replacements or buy them from someone else. Day

old chicks and point of lay pullets seem to be the two most usual options. You try everything during your long field tenure. The nearest neighbours are just far enough away not to be woken by your cockerel but he does wake you all, and it does not please everyone. Seeing tiny chicks scooting around and watching the mother hen syndrome in its original guise is totally captivating but there are problems. The cockerel seems to focus the attention of the entire local fox population on your farm. They patrol in pairs and despite your heroic efforts one fox succeeds in abducting the cockerel. A week later your husband finds his handsome red feet outside the foxes' earth.

Some people like to keep their hens at arm's length, which equates to an orchard, a field or a garden length. As long as they have plenty of room to enjoy themselves, unlimited access to pure water and suitable food they will be happy. However, all the hens you knew as a child, the hens you know now, and all the hens yet to come, actually like the society of people and you feel, therefore, that once you offer them the chance to be part of the family, you cannot subsequently banish them to the bottom of the garden. When hens play all day and consider going home synonymous with going to bed, they often do not run to the night quarters for shelter if it rains heavily. You always make sure that they have access to alternative shelter and are never allowed to become too wet or cold; a trauma, even if only a minor one can result in no eggs for several days.

Hens have more uses than just being good company and supplying you with eggs; they dig parts of the garden to a fine tilth and they eat slugs and other unwelcome guests. In the 'useful' category, pigs also feature strongly. Despite their intelligence falling short of that displayed by all your other livestock, they are powerful friends if you can harness or contain what otherwise could be a destructive force. They can dig deep and eradicate unwanted roots and weeds and have a wonderful time doing it; they think hard work is mere playtime. It is the 'containing' bit, which is the tricky bit.

Pigs do not play a central role in your farming activities; cows and hens are crucial, sheep are delightful and handy, pigs are occasional, interesting and useful if they stay at home. To begin with you buy a breeding sow. She is sweet natured and companionable. A couple of days before she farrows, she builds a nest. It is January and quite cold. She sets to work with a single-minded determination and nothing you say about impending storms, retarded occluded weather fronts or clouds that gather round the setting sun can deter her. She works hard, relentlessly gathering, of all things, stinging nettles; her nose and face are pink with the constant stinging. An enormous pile of nettles, twigs and grasses is accumulated, and finally, she stands back to admire her handiwork and then attempts to climb on top. She rolls off, like Teddy 'falling off the ottoman'. She climbs up again; she is a very large pig. All this time you are watching from a discreet distance. She almost certainly would not mind if you were to move in really close but you do not want to interrupt her timetable; she obviously knows exactly where she needs to be and when she needs to be there. As far as you can tell, this has to be instinctive behaviour; no pig has been around to teach her.

The next morning, after an unusually mild night, she produces eleven healthy piglets. The weather improves steadily for the next three weeks. They eat, sleep and make merry down by the stream and then it starts to rain. You both go with a large laundry basket and load the piglets for the short but leg-tiring journey up to the barn. The sow follows, presumably glad that you were on hand to play your part in the proceedings.

There will inevitably be many times during your life to come when you keep no pigs. If, after a gap of a few months or years, you find yourselves with a surplus of milk, buttermilk or whey, you might, on occasion, buy a couple of weaned piglets (weaners) from an organic smallholder in a nearby village.

Curing Bacon

Learning how to cure your bacon satisfactorily takes a number of attempts. You are inundated with contradictory advice. Your older neighbours enjoy telling you how they spent gruelling hours rubbing dry salt into flitches by hand in a pig lead, an item itself which is considerably more than just potentially lethal. By trial and error, as in most things you do, you arrive at a way of curing bacon that actually works. You grate salt which you buy in enormous lumps, freshly mined, of course, from those same ancient deposits in Cheshire, to avoid the addition of any so-called 'free-running' chemical; these compounds, it seems, can contain small amounts of cyanide, which sounds distinctly undesirable as a food additive. You then dissolve the salt in your spring water at the rate of one pound per gallon. This is then slowly heated to boiling point, stirring fairly often, and is then slowly cooled. When it is very cold you immerse the flitches and hams, hocks and trotters, taking care to turn them daily. The flitches are cured in five days and the hams in eight, slightly longer if the joints are thick. These items are then well swilled with pure water, hung on hooks to drain and are either sliced, cooked and eaten or frozen. No saltpetre is ever needed, as its role as a preservative, dangerous as it may be as an entity, is rendered unnecessary by the expediency of freezing.

If you find the ham too salty when you come to cook it this is easily remedied by discarding the water in which you first bring it to the boil, and replacing it with fresh. Over salty bacon can be washed in milk and dried before cooking or, for delicate constitutions, it can be entirely cooked in milk, in a shallow dish in an oven.

In all respects eggs make a welcome contribution to the organic recipes at your command so when, a number of years later, you feel your hens' egg producing inclinations are slowing down, you try to buy some organic, day old chicks. There are none to be found. The organic movement is still in its infancy. You feel sure that there must be some organically fed, if not officially accredited, chicks somewhere but tracking them down proves impossible. Instead you buy four point of lay pullets from a local free range flock and feed them on home grown everything; water, milk, meat, wheat, weeds, grass-to-graze, bread, cherries, raspberries, very soft apple and, of course, the freedom of large areas of freshly dug soil and the irresistible tiny life forms therein. They also feast carelessly on your precious foxgloves, having heard, presumably, that digitalis is good for the heart.

Somewhere along the road to your elusive goal of self-sufficiency you take the conscious decision to shed your once cherished wish to live without sugar. Various friends and relations come and go and several are not as healthy as you so you find yourself forever having to stretch your imagination to find food to tempt them. This sometimes means preparing virtually your whole armoury of easily digestible fare. One absolute favourite with the adults is meringue; not the usual light-as-air 'bon bouche' but a relatively heavy, solid, golden, delectable and satisfying item.

The details of the many deep-rooted health problems which gradually emerge as people stay for several days both worry and intrigue you. So many individuals look fine and only ever moan about small things during brief everyday meetings. Everyone tries to find a way of coping, often by excluding certain foods entirely. You are also rather surprised by how many people seem to ask for boiled water rather than tea.

The Best Milk in the World

You invariably make a point of offering a glass of milk. Roughly half accept but a few refuse with vigour. Some are tentative. After a time you change the words you use. Instead of saying "would you like a glass of milk?" you simply hand them a glass and say "would you like to try a glass of the best milk in the world?" This raises a smile and almost everyone risks a sip. Almost everyone smiles again and drinks with enthusiasm. A discourse always follows about how much they liked milk when they were young and how they never seem to drink it nowadays. You explain the difference and they listen.

Meringues

In a 1½ pint bowl you put three pinches of pure salt and the whites of two eggs, neither too new nor too old, perhaps some laid 5-7 days ago provided they have been kept cold. Whisk the mixture robustly until it begins to thicken, at which point you add 4 ounces of very finely ground organic sugar. Grinding it in a coffee grinder will produce the right result. Then tip it all in at one go while continuing to whisk quickly. You usually use Demerara but various organic sugars work equally well, each imparting its own particular flavour. Learning from the first debacle, when the cooling mechanism of the electric whisk blew much of the sugar all over the kitchen, you now take great care to tip it into the side of the bowl. Now you have also learnt from experience precisely when to stop whisking. The mixture should be soft but definitely not liquid; it will just form soft peaks as you remove the whisk.

Have ready two flat trays lined with unbleached baking paper. Scoop as much of the mixture on to a dessert spoon as you can without risking any falling off and carefully place it with a confident, throwing action into spoon-shaped objects on the tins, deftly lifting the spoon off with a hint of a twist. Cook, or more precisely, dry them in a cool oven overnight when the wood fire is just ticking over or when electricity is cheaper. Remove them from the oven the next morning, eight or so hours later, lifting the meringues immediately and placing them upside down on the baking tray until they are cold. This takes very little time. Finally, store them in an airtight container, puffing out any trapped air after fitting the lid.

Ice Cream

The two leftover egg yolks can be used in ice cream by making two tablespoonfuls of organic sugar as fine as icing sugar by grinding and pounding it, then beating the sugar with the two yolks until the mixture becomes frothy and then adding half a pint of stiffly whipped cream. This is put into an ice tray on maximum freeze until it is firm (about 4 hours later) and should be eaten the same day.

Over the years you have plenty of opportunities to find other uses for egg yolks. Real custard, either baked or as a sauce, is a strong contender and many recipes exist and they all seem to work. For one you beat 4 yolks with 1 tablespoon of honey and then slowly add half a pint of warm milk, whisking gently and constantly until it thickens. Sometimes you 'whizz' 2 yolks with 2 teaspoons of honey and a quarter of a pint of cream in a liquidiser and then pour this over a damson flan and bake it in the oven. But, from the day you acquire a double saucepan, you stir your custard with a wooden spoon. Egg yolks also thicken soups from time to time and they are of course needed to make marzipan.

Victoria Sponge made with Vinegar

You recall reading that 15ml (half a fluid ounce) of organic white wine vinegar could take the place of one egg in a cake recipe. You try it and the resulting cake is even better than usual. One day you have only egg yolks to spare and so you try a cake with yolks, vinegar and a teaspoon of cold water mixed to the right consistency. A basic Victoria sponge (4 oz of butter, 4 oz of sugar, 2 eggs and 4 oz of flour plus baking powder) works wonderfully with 6 egg yolks and a rather cavalier amount of vinegar measured more by the eye than scales. Large cakes too do not suffer at all from an absence of egg white.

Fruit Cakes

Two large and scrumptious fruit cakes once emerged from one pound of butter beaten to a whiteness with one pound of sugar, 18 egg yolks (after a meringue festival), the right amount of vinegar and milk, maybe a wine glass of each, perhaps more of the milk, two pounds of flour with a teaspoon of baking powder diligently mixed in and three pounds of washed and dried, dried fruit, approximately half sultanas and half raisins. You cooked these at 150 degrees for an hour and a half with your usual peering and testing instinct.

Once vinegar finds its way into your kitchen it makes itself a useful ally in a surprisingly large number of ways. Self-sufficient it is not, though potentially it could be, but its usefulness obliterates the need for many other potential purchases.

4.
Your Garden

By a combination of luck and good judgement, the hedges on what you insist on calling your 'farm' contain wild plums, hazelnuts and sloes. There are also two ancient walnut trees and the cherry, apples, pears, plums and mulberry you planted. The soft fruits are doing particularly well too. And then, of course, there are blackberries.

Blackberrying is both a verb and an unmissable tradition. You all pick enthusiastically from the very first tentative ripe berries in August until the frost puts paid to the fun. Quite often there are some to be found in early October, which the soft sun has warmed and ripened to an unusual sweetness and your ingenuity is most certainly called upon as you all try to reach the high-hanging clusters. You take them home and pile them all into a dish, letting fall on them an almost imperceptible puff of sugar to wake them up and then a goodly shower of fresh lemon juice to really bring them to life. You all help yourselves and most of you decide these late treats do not need the thick cream they justified earlier in the season. It is, in effect, a free meal but then all your food is free, or at least to cost it would be ludicrous: forty pounds a pint for milk, a hundred pounds per cheese, five pounds for a loaf of bread and blackberries picked at the rate of one pound an hour at the legal minimum wage. You give your time. It is the only thing you have to give.

You begin to enjoy this chosen life and harvesting is one of the many joys. However, after a couple of ideal years, a few problems arise. Slugs eat their way into the potatoes and lettuce, the late frost in May damages the blossom on the fruit trees, squirrels take every single nut and you begin to see the advantages of supermarkets. You battle on, but you cannot help thinking that humans are the only 'flies in the ointment'; there would be no problems at all if you did not want a share too.

Slugs

A friend comes to see you from Birmingham and assures you she is a seasoned gardener. She offers to remove the slugs from the brassica. You are so grateful you accept and she disappears before you think to offer advice. You have dough rising in various stages of readiness and forget all about her for several hours. Eventually she returns, triumphantly announcing that she has removed them all. You are just taking the bread out of the oven and are about to prepare a meal of baked potatoes, butter, accidental cheese, which she insists on trying and loves, ripe tomatoes warm from the greenhouse, lettuce you had managed to protect from the slugs with circles of soot and wood ash and tiny, sweet radishes grown to mark the rows of carrots and harvested before the carrots need the space.

You have to force her to eat because, as a rule, she eats nothing but bread and butter. She is one of your potentially unhealthy friends who looks and feels fine at the moment but, you fear, is storing up trouble for the future. She adores everything you give her but once she is at home she hates wasting time growing, cooking or eating anything which takes more than a couple of minutes. You make it your special project to mend her ways. People so rarely think about prevention until after something goes wrong. Animals, in contrast, perhaps do not think about it but certainly they spend their entire lives eating as judiciously as their circumstances allow, which means they are protecting and improving their immune systems and general health all the time.

After she has gone it occurs to you to wonder what she did with the slugs but as she is a practical person you imagine she will have done something sensible. You did not want to tell her that you always take them for a long walk and release them, hoping they will not crawl back to the garden, your husband kills any that he removes both neatly and humanely. Some months later, on a second visit, you ask her. She answers that she had not known what to do and had had the sensitivity not to ask and so, had put them in a bucket and taken them home to Birmingham They had then, relentlessly and repetitively, made their way up to the top of the bucket so she drove dangerously, reaching over to the passenger's side of the car to prize them off the rim and drop them back in the bottom of the bucket.

Thankfully, after a few more years, the garden settles down and develops an ability to cope. Each succeeding year the land becomes more alive as crops fight off pests and diseases and a balance is created between both pests and their natural predators. You step back and watch all the creatures interacting. The livestock are radiant and calm and you delight in watching the myriad life forms.

They all look so healthy; hedgehogs, frogs, toads, blue tits, all relentlessly pursuing their own goals and at the same time all benefiting your garden immensely. The huge variety of plants and your careful rotation of them round the garden, has created a happy environment. You never plant a single esoteric, exotic or minority interest vegetable as space is too limited. You are committed to self-sufficiency and not just a simple wish to grow some of your own food. You now grow potatoes, carrots, parsnips, beetroot, swede, many different brassicas, lettuce, tomatoes, onions, marrows, cucumbers and a very important, large bed of rhubarb. The soft fruit garden comprises strawberries, raspberries, blackcurrants and gooseberries.

One particular year, torrential rain washes many of your vegetables downstream towards the next village. You find yourself thinking about all the valuable topsoil you lost with them. You had read many years ago just how long it takes to produce a one inch layer of topsoil and had always been careful to keep the soil you had washed from your vegetables prior to cooking, returning it to the garden. It is the middle of August and now too late to replant but you have to risk it; a winter without potatoes would be dire. You hurriedly prepare a patch of ground, high up above the newly established water table, and plant five rows of King Edwards. You watch over them, earth them up and hoe the weeds simultaneously. And then come the nightly forecasts of ground frost. You all repair to the potato patch just before bedtime for a few, dangerous days and cover it with every cotton sheet, spare curtain and old thin towel you possess. Ten weeks later, having looked in vain for any sign of a flower, you tentatively, but with little real hope, search down into the friable soil and find a superb crop of buckshee potatoes.

Carrot and Parsnip Soup

Sometimes you make a large cauldron of soup so that there is always something for everyone to grab when there seem not to be enough hours of daylight to finish all the work. You all enjoy carrot and parsnip soup, which you make by quietly bubbling slices of carrot, parsnip and onion in butter in the ratio of roughly 8 carrots to 3 parsnips to 1 small onion. If you have any stock prepared this will be waiting to receive the vegetables, but you sometimes use the water in which you previously casseroled a joint of beef. Everything is simmered gently until required. If unexpected guests arrive you simply add water, boiled potatoes and sometimes whole, ripe tomatoes to make it stretch. Salt is added to suit individual tastes in the serving bowls. Your own wholemeal bread is the only appropriate accompaniment.

Lord Derby

Cox's orange pippin

Egremont Russet

Apples

One autumn there is a bumper crop of apples. These are Newton Wonders which you acquired in a bartering arrangement with a neighbour; he in turn acquired a regular supply of loaves and an intermittent supply of butter. Your own apple orchard will take a few more years to become productive but you are looking forward to harvesting such varieties as Worcester Permaine, Cox's Orange Pippin, Egremont Russet, Lord Derby, Bramley's Seedlings and Laxton Fortune, each with its own distinctive characteristics of flavour and texture and unique behaviour when cooked. You are determined to honour the tradition of never eating a Blenheim Orange before Christmas Day and then just one each, every day thereafter. You agonise over which varieties of pear to grow as there is such a bewildering choice with as many as eighty-six being grown in one English county alone. You also read and consult widely on the best methods of storage.

Mrs. Beeton's *Book of Household Management* says, 'The best mode of preserving apples is to carry them at once to the fruit room…'. As yet you lack an ideal 'fruit room,' but set about constructing a substitute. You tie thin, strong strings to the corners of a wooden pallet then you both ascend parallel ladders and manage to suspend the pallet platform from the rafters of the barn. You disappear for a few minutes to fetch boxes of apples but while your backs are turned the hens climb up one of the ladders, inspect the hanging platform, decide it is bedtime and take up residence. You return and look up to see where the singing is coming from and don't have the heart to evict the new tenants. You alter your plans, take a week to locate another pallet and hang this one in a different outhouse.

The rhubarb patch is tended with care. The first young shoots are so sweet they need nothing but a drop of pure water in which to be brought to a very brief boil. Subsequent pullings are variously poached, stewed or baked in pastry.

You cherish a wish to have a flower garden too and you begin in fine style as various relatives give you plants. Your parents contribute dahlias and roses, blue lilies and a peony which of course refuses to bloom for all of the next fifteen years. One pink phlox is already

47

seventy, a present from a former neighbour of ninety-six. Surreptitiously over the next few years, the flower garden starts to grow vegetables. Your husband tactfully plants a few Painted Lady runner beans, hoping that you will accept their delicate pink and white flowers as sufficiently aesthetic to grace the flower beds.

Soon you too join in and plant a grape vine on the south-facing wall. You study the cultivation instructions and stand back for a full five minutes, secateurs poised for action, until you realise you cannot prune it for a year. Five years later, while you have been milking and washing, making and baking, eating, sleeping, dreaming and, oh yes, reading, it has completely covered the garage roof, become irrevocably entwined with one of the clematis, which had been sent as a gift by a friend from Ireland, exquisitely well packed in a sawn-almost-in-half-and-therefore-hinged plastic bottle, and is now busy climbing up a holly bush.

The plants actually co-exist happily and, after another few years, almost everything is edible. You make large amounts of compost and have a good depth of old beech leaves to dig for, under the shallow rooted mast-bearers in whose shade the pigs forage.

Sloe and Apple Jelly

The first time you picked sloes was when you were still at primary school. Your mother had either found or invented a recipe for a jelly to rival cranberries to accompany the Christmas turkey. The sloes looked lovely; dull, dark blue and softly ripe. It was the middle of October. You had been warned not to eat one but you could not resist and had regretted it for the next twenty-five years; the exact impact of the dry, sour taste staying with you undiminished. Nonetheless, you helped to make the jelly using equal quantities of sloes and sweet apples, probably Worcester Permaines, placed in a large jam kettle and cooked gently until soft. A four-pound total of fruit needed two pints of pure water. The cooked fruit was then tipped into a muslin cloth or jelly bag and suspended from a beam and the juice which issued forth was collected in a bowl.

You can remember vividly being told never to squeeze the bag for fear of making the clear, maroon liquid cloudy. Today, in your own home and in your own chosen life you reconsider this, squeeze the bag, obtain another cup full of juice and delight in the fact that no-one seems to notice the appearance but merely revels in the taste. It seems impossible to you to work out how to make jam or jelly without sugar. Something inside you cannot help feeling it is nobler to use only honey and this ideological tussle never completely goes away. In the end you compromise yet again and use both.

Twelve ounces of sugar were added per pint of juice, the mixture was then boiled until the setting point was reached, and you had then, as you have now, an excitingly delicious conserve. Although crab apples are decorative and provide a happy display if left on the tree, a few pounds, picked and made as above, can be a treat not to be under estimated. The result could actually be described as crab apple concrete as the high pectin content which helps it to set so firmly also means that it has to be virtually sliced from the jar.

At some time in the future you discover *Elinor Fettiplace's Receipt Book* dated 1604 and not published for almost three centuries thereafter, and you cannot stop reading it. You find that 'receipt' after 'receipt' not only accords with your own home-grown ingredients but also contributes enormously to your ability to use and preserve them. Thinking, as you are at this moment about fruit jelly, you follow the directions for 'Printed Red and White Apple Jelly,' marvelling that a pound of apples, unpeeled and cooked uncovered, will produce an absolutely clear jelly, while the same weight of the same apples, but peeled and cooked with a closely fitting lid, will miraculously supply jelly of a stained glass window red.

5.
Sloes & the Forgotten Fruit

You find that your resolve to make bread every day lasts for little more than a fortnight, at which point you are irresistibly drawn to pillaging the memory of yet one more elderly farmer's wife. You arrive by prior arrangement in the early evening. Supper has just been cleared away and a daughter-in-law has covered the table with layers of blankets and sheets and is ironing. She takes little part in the conversation but irons continually. Everyone in the household looks crisp and pristine but you are unable to take your eyes off her as her iron sails through blouses and shirts, trousers and skirts and on and on through towels, underwear and socks.

The farmer's wife lends you the not-yet-published

manuscript of a cookery book she started a long time ago and you go home and read:

"For availability and versatility, look no further than The Yellow Pershore Egg Plum. Many old orchards have been awash with acres of these trees for generations, covered from their topmost tip with ripening fruit cascading down to the orchard grass, and most of it studiously ignored. It is almost impossible to find a plum to eat, worth the effort of picking, and most people walk straight past to the nearest Victoria tree, but when it comes to cooking there is no finer or more valuable fruit than the Pershore Plum; fresh or frozen these are a resource to be treasured."

A Delicious Pudding with Plums

For an easily prepared and delicious pudding which will literally cook itself while you are out working, choose 4-6 plums per person, slit them open lengthways and remove the stones. Place them, cut side uppermost, in an ovenproof dish in a single layer. Sprinkle them with organic Demerara sugar or dot them with honey and place the dish in the plate-warming drawer (or equivalent low temperature oven) They will be ready to eat, either with or without cream, whenever you come back. For every hour they are left cooking the taste and consistency will change, turning from firm, barely cooked plums, through soft sweetness to caramel-like delectability, eventually becoming something resembling toffee before shrivelling to oblivion, if you are detained by a procrastinating cow, or its equivalent.

Over the next few years, having secured an indefinite supply from an orchard owner as yet unenlightened as to the virtues of these golden plums, you set about getting to know them by both inventing and accumulating recipes.

A Scrumptious Pudding

By now you are making bread with your own home-grown, home milled flour on a daily basis and occasionally make a bit of enriched dough by rubbing 4 ounces of butter into one pound of flour and adding 3 ounces of sugar before adding the yeast which you dissolve in milk. When half risen for the second time, after being rolled out to fit a large baking tin, you cover the dough with a crumble mixture of 8 ounces of flour, 3oz of butter (rubbed in) and 3oz of sugar and then decorate it with cut, stoned plums, placing them cut side down. It is then baked for approximately 30 minutes at 400 degrees Fahrenheit, 200 degrees Celsius. Experience will eventually enable you to prepare this scrumptious pudding at just the right moment to be popped in the oven as soon as the bread is taken out.

Many of the published recipes you found told you to use apricots, taking no account whatever of buying local or the virtues of self-sufficiency. You discover by trial and error, however, that it is perfectly satisfactory to use frozen plums. This is both a relief, because the instinct to hoard overcame you entirely when you were picking plums in the autumn, and a cause for feeling guilty because the plum glut encouraged you to buy a freezer with its attendant CO_2 emissions and electrical dependence and you have not yet succeeded in generating a single amp from wind, water or leg power. You do, however, remain confident for the rest of your life that you will eventually one day be able to sit on a stationary bike and pedal sufficient kilowatts to power at least one light bulb.

You find that when using frozen plums, the stones can be removed with a sharp knife and extreme care, just a few minutes after removing them from the freezer. The skins slip off easily at this stage too and this is useful as the skins tend to taste bitter after they have been frozen. Frozen plums stew beautifully, and bake well on dough but they tend to collapse and look a bit brown when cooked slowly in an oven. Timing is all when dealing with frozen plums.

You occasionally use an alternative topping for the enriched dough by spreading the half risen dough with: a couple of tablespoonfuls of cottage cheese mixed with an egg yolk and a spoonful of sugar, and finishing with a final layer of halved plums. This takes slightly longer to cook at a slightly higher temperature.

Pershore Plums

The recipe book you borrowed tells you that the best

jam in the world, universally liked and with myriad uses, is made from hard, green Pershore plums, gathered before the main crop is picked. If you are an expert jam-maker, it says, you need no advice here but if you are incredibly short of time, then you can freeze whole plums and make batches of jam later. With frozen plums it is time-consuming to remove the stones. By far the quickest option is to make the jam with the stones in; they are easy to remove as you come to eat it, either on bread and butter or in other dishes.

Welsh Cheese Cakes

The most exciting little cakes in which this jam should be used are euphemistically called Welsh Cheese Cakes. Make the pastry the night before or at least a few hours in advance; you will only need a tiny quantity for 12 small cakes. You rub one ounce of butter into two and a half ounces of wholemeal flour and add sufficient cold water to form a ball; this must be much wetter than you would need for a white flour pastry. It almost sticks to your hands, but not quite. Place it in a plastic bag (self-sufficiency ideals coming apart again) and leave it in the fridge overnight, where it will continue to absorb the liquid.

When you are ready to line the patty pans warm up the pastry slightly until it is sufficiently pliable to roll out. Cut out 12 rounds. Once cut, gently roll out each individual round again to very minutely increase its area, thus making the pastry even thinner. The pastry needs to be thin so that it cooks at the same rate as the cake topping, although we are not quite talking about Strudel thinness.

For the cake mixture beat 2 ounces of butter with 2

ounces of sugar, adding one egg and 2 ounces of flour containing a pinch of baking powder. Place a teaspoon of Pershore Plum Jam in each pastry case. Then divide the cake mixture equally, popping a portion on top of the jam. Cook this for approximately 15 minutes at 320°F (160°C), allow them to cool just slightly before eating, although they are lovely eaten cold too.

Simply stewing these 'golden wonders' makes a delicious and easy pudding and you find that plum juice, thus cooked, is gorgeous with porridge: just a single teaspoonful in the bottom of the bowl makes all the difference. The fruit is also equally good with a batter mixture (4oz of wholemeal flour, a pinch of salt, 1 egg and half a pint of milk) cooked in the oven. In this oven pancake, the heavy flour sinks as it cooks, forming a pastry-like base and the milk and egg form a quiche-like topping. It is really a Yorkshire pudding served up as a dessert. Sugar and lemon juice, in true pancake-style, are also good here too.

It is possibly too casual to say 'simply stewing' as, over the years, you find that getting the exact ratio of water to sugar to fruit is absolutely critical; too much of one, too little of another or over or under cooking, can change the result immeasurably. You find that the ratio to be arrived at is peculiar to the person eating it and varies as widely as the recipes you have found for making comfrey ointment.

As Pershore plums appear in such huge quantities, you keep on finding new uses for them and often mix them stewed with other fruit like raspberries, gooseberries and blackcurrants. To your great delight you think of a way of using the frozen strawberries which you can never resist freezing when in over abundance.

You arrange them round the edge of a pastry flan case while still frozen solid, fill the middle with stewed, mixed fruit, boil up the liquid with arrowroot or its wild counterpart, kuzu, and encapsulate the frozen strawberries in the hot liquid, ensuring that the strawberries retain their shape and flavour as they thaw. Usually the mixed fruit contains dark coloured berries like blackcurrants or raspberries, but occasionally you only choose plums and gooseberries so that the strawberries are enclosed in a clear glaze and their own colour predominates.

Suet Pudding

You decide that, once you have come to grips with meat production and therefore have some suet at your disposal, you will treat yourself to a boiled suet pudding and dream about lining a basin with suet pastry (6 ounces of flour, 3 ounces of grated suet plus a good pinch of salt, all mixed with cold water) filling it with plums, adding honey to taste and steaming it for at least 2 hours. You also think far enough ahead to envisage locking the door before you start eating it or you might have to share it with a neighbour, irresistibly drawn towards the aroma.

Traditionally your mother and your grandmother would have used apricot jam to secure the almond paste to a fruit cake prior to icing; Pershore Plum jam is an ideal substitute. Also, when you were growing up, the icing was white. Now, grinding organic raw cane or Demerara sugar finely in a coffee grinder, you produce icing sugar that is a varying shade of gold. The only problem is that you grow neither almonds nor sugar, but are more than content to eat un-iced cake. Traditional fruitcake ought to be off the menu too as you cannot devise a substitute for organic dried fruit. In the end, you find yourself buying organic dried fruit once a year for a batch of Christmas cakes and puddings to satisfy, or perhaps mollify, the various givers of ancient and treasured recipes. At a slightly later date you inadvertently produce your own almonds. You are given what you are told is a peach tree. You plant it, tend it and train it to grow on the wall of the house. Tiny fruits then form and, as you eagerly anticipate peaches, you in fact receive almonds.

Christmas Pudding

The Christmas pudding recipe you all like best contains 5 ounces of wholemeal, freshly ground flour, 8 ounces of suet grated on a cheese grater, 4 ounces of breadcrumbs, 11 ounces of sultanas, 11 ounces of raisins, 4 ounces of organic sugar, the grated rind and the juice of one of your own lemons, 3 of your own eggs and your own milk to mix. You generally triple this recipe as these puddings keep so well.

The mixture must be moist, verging on the very moist, as the flour continues to absorb the liquid during cooking. It is transferred to a buttered Pyrex bowl, covered with a lid made of buttered, unbleached greaseproof paper and a second lid made of muslin or a thin cotton tea towel (organic cotton of course), secured with string and either placed in a steamer or a saucepan containing an inch of boiling water and is cooked for two hours. A further hour's cooking will be needed just prior to eating.

You find that you get into the habit of saying that you cannot make any suet pudding without a torch; this is because you have to peer in quite frequently at the water level to make sure it does not boil dry.

6.
Work

You resolved to stop learning/enjoying yourself/
wasting time and start 'doing'. You donned a pair
of dungarees, pushing from your mind the depressing
knowledge that you bought rather than made them,
and climbed on to the half finished roof of your house.
Your husband smiled and handed you a hammer and
a gorgeous, tough, cloth bag full of nails, which you
clipped on to your belt. He explained what to do and
left you on a safe piece of scaffolding while he ascended
like a sure-footed mountain goat to the apex. You had
plenty of time to reflect on how he managed to find the
time to make the bag, grow the vegetables, milk the cow

and construct the house. You threw yourself wholly into self-sufficient living. Little did you realise at the time that neither of you would have another day off for the rest of your lives. But hard work proves far more therapeutic than you ever imagined and learning new skills of necessity, is truly a delight. The years pass and you milk once a day, giving your cow no concentrated food but rather apples, sweet hay and a good grooming.

Making Butter

You strain the milk through fine muslin and leave it to cool in large, wide, shallow bowls. Twenty-four hours later you skim off the thickest cream to make into butter. Your laudable efforts to use an antique wooden churn fail and you resort to an electric device. Every day, your dream of living self-sufficiently takes yet another knock and you try to come to terms with a hard, healthy, fulfilling, semi-self-sufficient life of compromise.

You continue for many more years eschewing tea and coffee and making fruit juices and herbal beverages. You cling to the comforting knowledge that you have pure air and water, your own milk and wheat, quite an array of fruit and vegetables but there are still so many things you cannot make, but you remain determined to do your best.

For a long time after you had found your field, life had its own delicious pace. You were in quite an isolated position and you rose with the sun and went to bed just after it did. Every day was bursting with activity and you drank water and air, ate walnuts, blackberries, apples and pears and tasted freedom and tranquillity. You were soon able to start eating some of the vegetables you had planted too, mostly raw. Although you slept in a tiny caravan until your house was finished, it felt more like camping or living wild.

Nettles

Early on you had to make a psychological leap and embrace the idea of liking stinging nettles. This was not easy. When you were still at school you had climbed a willow tree to pick gooseberries from a parasitically attached bush and you had fallen out of the tree into a blackberry bush embellished with stinging nettles. No one at school believed that you had fallen out of a gooseberry bush. If they had, it would have mitigated the effect of the nettle rash, which lasted for days. For many years thereafter you had not a good word to say for them. Your husband finds them entirely beneficial and eventually wins you round. He likes to snip off very young nettles in spring to cook and he has always been a keen identifier of butterflies, some of whose life cycles depend on nettles. A thick, tall wall of nettles

soon surrounds the vegetable garden, providing free lepidoptera housing and an effective wind-break. Patches of nettles appear in the pasture too. At certain seasons the cow eats them with a vengeance. Cosmetic perfection in both field and garden slip yet further down the agenda before falling off it completely. The wish to avoid it is, after all one of many reasons you have for giving supermarkets a wide berth.

'Wooding' is a verb entirely unknown to any dictionary but in daily use in your neck of the woods. Equally unacknowledged as having a past participle is the verb (and noun) 'sneck.' Every gate has a 'sneck' to keep it closed, and once it is closed it has been 'snecked;' somehow this information has been kept secret from dictionary compilers. A Scottish friend pronounces it 'snecket,' so you cheerfully admit to total ignorance about its correct, nay mythical spelling. An onomatopoeic dictionary would solve the dilemma.

The Wood Stack

At certain times of the year, various trees throw down perfect kindling; ash and walnut are particularly generous in this respect. If you collect it, you are 'wooding.' You are also 'wooding' when gathering slightly larger fallen limbs, which you then subsequently saw into log lengths. If you fail to pick up the proffered kindling, after a while it disappears. You store the wood in stacks and soon have dry stacks, green stacks, seasoned stacks and about-to-disintegrate stacks, though the wood in these is usually left behind for the beetles, of which you have many species. Each day you try to replenish what the fire eats.

Beech wood logs burn bright and clear,
if the wood is kept a year,
but ash wet or ash dry,
is fit for a queen to warm her slippers by.

These words from an anonymous poem have been part of your upbringing; it is only now as a field occupant that you realise their full significance. The wood burner provides heat for cooking, a constant supply of hot water and a friendly room temperature as well as keeping the lemon trees safe from frost and you are determined to feed it, without felling a single living tree. The open fire in the living room appreciates wood that does not spit hot embers onto the crudely but dynamically woven woollen rugs; for this fire you use hazel, holly, apple, cherry, pear, plum, maple and thorn, though ash and oak reign supreme. Willow and poplar are indeed truly awful, but they still go in the wood burner nonetheless.

Other verbs to have evaded inclusion in the closed shop of dictionary compilation are are: To 'blart;' the sound of a calf imperiously calling its mother. To 'bunt;' a calf encouraging its mother to let her milk down, by bashing her udder with its head (the calf equivalent of massaging or pummelling). To 'bather;' a hen having a dust bath.

Soon after you move in to your wonderful new house you incidently have a couple of children. These little adjuncts fit perfectly in to your ideal plan for self-sufficient living. They are totally happy playing in the orchard while you pick the fruit. They eat well and grow strong and healthy. It is not until they start secondary school that your lifestyle is seriously challenged.

The routine jobs have, by now, become so integral a part of your life that you no longer think of them as jobs; in the same way that you breathe without thinking, you simply move from job to job. You throw open the window each morning and assess the weather. As soon as it is safe, one of you liberates the hens from their fox-free night quarters. For their part they would be happy to come out much earlier but only when one of you is working or playing outside, making a noise of some kind, do you feel the hens will be totally safe. The fox also exhibits a constant fascination for the wild ducks which visit your pond, but it shows no interest whatever in the moorhens, although you can be pretty certain that if they are strolling, or more often scurrying around proprietorially, the fox is not near.

You all have round the clock fresh air to breathe and always leave a small chink of window open in the bedrooms, even on the coldest nights. Maybe this was what caused the peacock butterfly to wake up and flutter her escape attempt one cold, wet, December day. There was a fierce east wind and pouring rain. She still wished to escape. You brought honey and water and syrup but they were ignored. You then walked out in the Wuthering gale and searched the garden; it was almost dark. You came back with a spray of flowering jasmine, caught the butterfly and placed her on a tempting, yellow flower. She actually emanated happiness and, after a three-course-meal or the equivalent, tucked herself into the fold of a cool curtain for a long sleep. You all felt elated.

One of you always milks the cow by hand, either once or twice a day, and the knowledge you need to decide which, comes with experience. The milk goes in to a stainless steel bucket, taking whatever the cow can contentedly spare, any calf always coming first, but that's only fair. On the days when there is plenty of milk, the prospect of making butter twice a week has to be planned for. It is difficult to dedicate the necessary time to hard cheese production, and you have to accumulate milk from several days in order to have enough to make a large enough cheese to mature well but it is a wonderful way of storing milk safely. You do, however, make soft cheese quite frequently.

Collecting eggs is everyone's favourite job and the children accompany you from a very early age. There is a special basket, referred to with considerable imagination as the egg basket, which is always used to carry the eggs safely home. At the age of four your first child asks to be allowed to collect the eggs unaccompanied. You agree but watch discreetly all the time. The diminutive person toddles down the orchard, negotiating thigh high grass and holding the basket aloft. It is the time when you have quite a large flock and it just happens to be the first day they really get into their stride and there are almost twice as many eggs as the day before. You gradually find out what happened, in fits and starts of disjointed and excited conversation with the child, who was evidently extremely perplexed to find more eggs than the basket would hold but, knowing that eggs always went in that basket, diligently persisted in placing them in, even though one or more rolled off simultaneously. Every egg collected had been counted with care, though it was a double-edged compensation to know exactly how many had been lost. You also knew, but of course did not say, that the child could only count to twenty haltingly, and from that point usually began at one again.

7.
The King Edward Potato

By a happy accident you meet the founder of what comes to be known as Garden Organic. Lawrence Hills and his wife Cherry sweep in to your lives, teaching you more important things about life, living and growing than you had learnt in all your previous afternoons put together. It is the day of their twenty-fifth wedding anniversary. Cherry is a physiotherapist and an intuitive healer who bubbles with energy. Having survived fifty unhappy years in her first marriage, she is now making the most of her second. She seems to know how to help people and makes you all feel better. She knows many exercises which she teaches you, including a beautiful arm grip which you learn and use on each other. She grasps your left hand with her left and grips your left elbow firmly with her right hand. She gently twists the hand outwards as she turns the elbow inward. It is all very subtle but conveys a deep feeling of well-being.

Lawrence enhances your knowledge of the properties of comfrey and also relates a fascinating tale about when The King Edward potato became effectively illegal. You are intrigued. In essence you seem to remember it was all about seed companies wanting people to buy new seed so they could charge royalties on it. Somehow or other they managed to get legislation passed making it illegal to sell King Edwards, even to a neighbour. Thinking back, you suppose that other varieties may have been affected too. There was, understandably, an outcry, resulting in a successful campaign to reverse this mad situation.

Seed Potatoes

You try growing many different types of potato over the years but realise that you all much prefer King Edwards. You vow to keep enough seed potatoes each year to keep you supplied in perpetuity. You succeed in this and, for the same reason, you always keep runner bean seeds too. Other seeds are trickier and you usually resort to buying them. As you get older, sourcing organic seeds becomes easier and Lawrence's organisation, originally called The Henry Doubleday Research Association, then The Organic Gardening Centre and now Garden Organic, plays a crucial role by the creation of its seed bank of organic vegetables.

You had largely forgotten all the legal pitfalls you had read about, but planting seed potatoes brings back not only this memory but also several others. Much of what you had read about self-sufficiency and small-scale farming was written long ago; it is a constant source of woe to be brought face to face with so many new and inexplicable regulations governing what you can and cannot do. You can remember a particular feeling of cynicism when the details of a much trumpeted act of parliament, purporting to tighten pesticide regulations, were eventually published. Far from making it easier for a member of the public suffering accidental contamination by a pesticide to find out the name and composition of the chemical in question, the new law actually gave more protection to the manufacturers and users. The power wielded by the chemical companies extended even to an allotment sized plot and the implications of following the letter of the law would have been laughable had they not been so sinister. For example, soap and water was effectively made illegal for home use as an insecticide, but if you could innocently claim that you were merely washing your plants you would have committed no offence.

What you really want is to be as self-sufficient and as isolated from authoritarian government and its attendant red tape as possible, and in your heart you knew before you started that it would prove an impossible dream. You had absorbed the experiences of Thoreau; he had managed to be self-sufficient and self-reliant to a degree to which you could never aspire. You particularly liked the way he described being too busy to read:

"I kept Homer's Iliad on my table through the summer, though I looked at his page only now and then. Incessant labor with my hands, at first, for I had my house to finish and my beans to hoe at the same time,

made more study impossible. Yet I sustained myself with the prospect of such reading in the future.'

You work even harder but learn to compromise with more grace. It is becoming clearer by the day that you cannot divorce yourself from what is generally described as the real world. To you it is the exact opposite; the artificial world. You can and do manage without a television but, although your field is of an indeterminate acreage and in an unspecified location, you still receive demands for council tax; it is proving impossible to live without money.

Your children are growing up and you decide to educate them at home; you are both qualified and easily obtain permission to do this. It is not long before you begin to receive pleas from other parents to teach their youngsters too. You have suddenly been handed an opportunity to both earn money and stay at home. You cannot afford to refuse. Most jobs have to be fitted in, but teaching requires planning, preparation and organisation. You start by teaching on alternate days but soon change to alternate weeks as coming in, getting changed and throwing off your farming persona takes time.

Every day is alluringly different but every task you undertake seems to be moving you in the right direction; digging and feeding the soil, planning the rotation, buying the seeds, tying in raspberry canes, weeding and watering all form part of a constant rhythm. Water butts are installed in every likely and unlikely place in what will become known one day as water harvesting but you cannot know this for another few decades.

All the preparatory work gets done, sometimes 'en famille,' sometimes solo, but when it comes to harvesting, everything seems to be ready simultaneously and a great effort is needed to lift, pick, cut and store. There is often very little energy left for eating.

As a general rule, all your livestock roam freely and happily coexist, but you occasionally need to intervene when young calves go through a phase of sheep chasing. If the sheep are heavily pregnant, they simply do not want such exercise or fear. If the lambs have already been born, the youngsters of both species can compete with, or ignore each other admirably.

Contact with children who own televisions and computers has an influence on your own children and the materialism you had fled creeps back into your lives. You are slightly alarmed to discover that your tiny, home-made babies quickly develop opinions of their own and the skill to argue against any and every argument you try to concoct to safeguard them from what you genuinely consider to be corrupting influences. Money becomes more and more essential and the purchase of a car is precipitated by the frightening realisation that you might not be able to act quickly enough in an emergency. To your joint chagrin, it eventually becomes necessary for one of you to work away from the farm, in order to be able to live there still.

Life is not going according to plan.

8.
Meat

Producing and using your own meat is a big hurdle to overcome. From a dietary and philosophical point of view, you both decide you want to eat meat. You have read, discussed and researched vegetarian and vegan ideals but, although immensely attracted by them, you decide you want to be omnivores, as long as you can produce the meat yourselves.

For one thing, you love seeing cattle, sheep, pigs and hens enjoying themselves. You assume that a vegan world would be devoid of domesticated animals, or they would be confined to areas where a few people could afford to keep them as ornaments. For the time being the sort of traditional agriculture you try to emulate relies on animals to supply the fertility to grow crops. You take every opportunity to talk to people about the practicalities involved in being a self-sufficient vegan or vegetarian. None of the ones you meet is able to grow what they feel they need for a healthy diet; indeed many of what they consider to be essential ingredients come from remote foreign parts. Most of these you have never even heard of. By abstaining from eating meat many people have also encountered serious deficiency symptoms. You keep an open mind on the virtues and practicalities of stockless systems.

Your determination to drink your own milk inevitably leads to your house cow producing calves and not all of the calves are female. When they reach two years of age, the male calves are slaughtered and you have every imaginable cut of beef plus liver, kidneys and suet. You have to face up to the fact that, as you and your bovines get older, you will have to choose between replacing an aging cow and slaughtering one of her daughters. You begin to see a strong argument forming in favour of owning a large farm so that you have room to keep every animal. Financial restraints prevent the daydreaming from lasting too long.

The affection and deep respect you all develop for your cows makes you feel part of a largely invisible, though tangible brotherhood. Nelson Mandela wrote in his autobiography: "I was no more than five when I became a herd boy, looking after sheep and calves in the fields. I discovered the almost mystical attachment that the Xhosa have for cattle, not only as a source of food and wealth, but as a blessing from God and a source of happiness." Adrian Bell in The Cherry Tree wrote about the character Joe Boxted who had a "single, lovely, gentle Alderney cow for whose well-being he would starve the whole farm, his wife and himself." These are only two of many similar sentiments from people both past and yet to come.

Beef Tea

Beef tea is one recipe you have been connected with since childhood; a nourishing and easily digested, pleasant-tasting beverage which your mother made and gave to anyone who needed it. As always, recipes adapted down through the ages as memories became unwittingly unreliable but shin, rump steak and shoulder certainly all make nourishing beef tea. Chopping the chosen meat into very small chunks presents more cut surfaces and more available albumen, which is the most beneficial element in the meat and closely resembles the white of an egg in its properties. The leftover meat chunks are pretty tasteless but are very tender and you can find many ways of incorporating them into different dishes. The hens adore them, which makes you pause for a few seconds to wonder whether hens actually have any taste buds at all; you never succeed in answering this to your satisfaction but decide it does not really matter.

A source of constant fascination is watching the hens' ability to decide, in an imperceptible fraction of a second, whether a proffered substance is even worth investigating, let alone eating. They stand alone amongst your livestock, humans included, in this respect. Cows, pigs, sheep and people all take a quick look. Cows always consider eating a new food item before deciding not to. Pigs eat almost everything but they certainly retain open minds and give due consideration to any new article, as do sheep and people, but hens, if offered something they do not intend to eat, will not even glance in its direction before declining.

The small pieces of meat, weighing in total one pound, are covered with one pint of cold, pure water and cooked gently in a closed casserole in the oven. Recipes vary, and cooking this in a water jacket or bain-marie is often suggested. Cooks disagree about how much salt to use and at what point to add it. In the end you believe it is best to cook it simply and add salt when it is eaten. If the temperature exceeds 130 degrees Fahrenheit the albumen coagulates and is subsequently lost when the tea is strained prior to serving. You are as confident of the quality of your beef as you are of your milk and do not feel the need to boil or pasteurise. It would be a very different story with produce of unknown origin. You read:

'The power of beef tea is hard to explain scientifically; it contains very little nourishment compared to the apparent good effect it has. It might belong to a new dimension of remedies.'

For as far back as you can remember there has been a general acceptance of the fact that liver from pigs or lambs is superior to that from beef animals. This is not so. Many people never venture near another slice of liver after leaving school, with unshakeable memories of the tough, inedible liver served there. You find that ox liver is sweet and tender and mild, if it comes from one of your own animals, properly fed.

Many things can go wrong and many things do. Some of these things are delightful, if unexpected deviations from what you might anticipate. One day, as you approach the bottom of the field near the stream, you see what your

mind interpretes as 'twin calves dotted all over the field.' You stand still, amused and shocked. Two, tiny, black entities are lying 30 and 50 yards from their mother as if they had belonged there for ever. A dictionary definition of forever might well equal the whole of one's life, so they have, indeed, been there forever; they are at most four hours old. Their mother is grazing unconcernedly. Some calves spend a few days being a bit unsteady and/or sleeping a great deal. Others, like these twins, instantly adopt the Mayfly's attitude to getting on with the one-day-whole-of-their-lives. The mother has plenty of milk for them but not a drop to spare for you. Luckily you have a second house cow by now.

Many years in the future a very different problem arises and one cow is frightened by foxhounds taking a short cut through your field. This results in her calving prematurely. Her milk supply takes a few days to catch up with events, and in the meantime you have to milk another cow, and give most of her milk to her friend's new calf. Both cows know you so well that they obviously expect you to solve such problems.

Lambing

Your small flock of sheep produces lambs and you have to decide how many ewe lambs you can keep. Sheep recognise and remember people, as well as other sheep, of course. This is one of a multitude of reasons you have for not leaving them in the care of anyone not known to them. You begin your flock with two orphan ewe lambs, then, a little while later, you are given another single one. The single lamb is a happy, self-sufficient entity with a good memory. She is delivered to you by her owner, just two hours after being born, having had one small feed of colostrum. Six weeks later, he calls to see you unexpectedly, and the lamb immediately recognises him. He is amazed and obviously quite moved.

In the beginning, your very first cow arrives equipped with one metal ear tag. At various dates later on, the rules are changed and her descendants find themselves needing two, one of which has to be 'distance readable,' washable, plastic and probably yellow.

Tags and Passports

In addition to the two ear tags, each bovine eventually has a passport and you receive BCMS Booklets 1-10, plus a stock-keeper's handbook, a herd record book, movement book and barcode labels. Twice each year you receive a cattle statement telling you how many bovines you have, how many have been born or have died since the previous statement, whether any have been moved and the dates on which some or all or none of these things happened. You apply for a holding number after which you receive a Holding Registration Document. You read every leaflet from cover to cover. If the EU or British Government decides to change any rules you receive Interim Guidance Rules. Wherever the cow goes, the passport must accompany her. When she leaves for her final journey or, if for any, inconceivable reason you sell her before then, she will not only take her passport with her but you will have to send a postcard to BCMS telling them where she has gone, with the date, your signature and a barcode label. You will almost certainly die with a large number of unused barcode labels in your possession.

You feel extra glad that you have a fairly ordinary Welsh Black cow when you are casually informed that, should you wish to buy a pedigree Jersey cow, she will have to have her portrait sketched by an artist within a week of being born. Furthermore, you discover that, were you to be inclined to want to breed a pedigree calf from her, you would have to hire a pedigree Jersey bull. From what little you know about Jersey bulls you feel it is quite likely you would not live long enough to find an artist to sketch the resulting calf.

Your sheep ultimately need one ear tag each, though the threat of two is constantly under discussion. By the time your children are bona fide farmers and you are starting to creak, you have to write out a movement license if you need to move them. You maintain a flock record book with a running total that must be filled in by the end of January each year. Pigs do not need ear tags, but they do need a movement licence to come to or leave your farm and, before you ever buy one, you will need permission to become a registered pig keeper. Several decades later the government will offer to pay you not to keep pigs or sheep or cows but fortunately you do not know this yet. Looking on the bright side, if you decide never to move anything it will certainly halve the paperwork.

You discover that sheep are highly intelligent, solving problems before your very eyes, and probably behind your back also. They demonstrate a certain compassion. On one occasion when you injure your knee, rushing as usual and bashing it into a metal post, one of the sheep stops grazing and walks over to where you are hopping around in agony. She stares at you in an undeniably concerned manner and, once you have become motionless, she gently rests her head on your leg, all the while looking directly at your face. Not until you manage to control your voice back to its normal pitch and assure her you are all right, does she resume her occupational grazing.

Another demonstration of ovine intelligence surprises and amuses you all. In a year when the grass is slow to grow back after haymaking, you give the sheep a couple of apples each day and a little hay with a big armful of willow. One day you forget to take the willow. You stand watching and talking to them as they eat their apples and a two-month old lamb marches over to the leafless willow twigs of the day before, picks one up and shakes it.

The importance of Grass

Keeping cows and sheep is not only a pleasure but also an integral part of your farming system. Interestingly and importantly, these ruminants graze grass and browse on leaves, which occur naturally and are free. They are equipped to convert grass into protein with supreme efficiency. Not only does this fact satisfy certain moral criteria; they are not consuming grain, which people can then eat, but the resulting milk and meat impart an enormous health benefit; the meat is higher in poly-unsaturated fats and contains essential amino acids, many of which are absent from a grain fed animal. Researchers have published findings which include the facts that grass fed beef contains 400% more Vitamin A, 300% more Vitamin E, 75% more omega-3 and 78% more Beta-carotene, as well as 500% more CLA, which you knew already.

Pigs, you decide, are much less clever than cows, sheep or hens, much more selfish, considerably more expensive to feed and far more destructive. They need large quantities of grain and, although they enjoy some grass, they need to be given additional protein. You would have several options if you were to buy protein, but as you want to produce it, you feel the two best options are milk or pulses. Your attempts to grow sufficient peas and beans are doomed to failure; mice eat every single pea in the trench before thay have a chance to start growing. You settle for milk as the protein component of your pigs' diet. This means, of course, that you can only keep pigs when you have milk to spare and milk to spare means no cheese and no butter. So you cannot have bacon and butter your bread; the king in A.A.Milne's *The King's Breakfast* would have sympathised.

First Buy a Field

You are beginning to think that all the problems of trying to become self-sufficient have one thing in common: you always have to compromise. At least you can achieve the only true goal you had set yourselves by allowing the animals in your care to live stress free, happy and interesting lives and actually being there for them is a crucial part of the bargain. One of you always takes them personally to the abattoir so that they can hear a familiar voice until the end. When you first started farming/cultivating your field, the legal requirements and red tape were comprehensible, even reasonable, and there were hundreds of small abattoirs performing an efficient, humane and vital service. Then everything became much harder. More than eight hundred small abattoirs were forced to close because of disastrously ill thought-out legislation. Regulations, record keeping and legal obligations made you both: incredulous, depressed, morose, bad tempered and defeatist. Well, almost. The future of your home produced meat rests on the proximity of an abattoir. You cannot and will not allow any animal to travel too far.

Stress

Your husband has a pretty well developed instinct, but he adores scientific facts. He finds yet another fascinating article and yes, he does find it on the Internet. Having survived, outwardly unscathed to the age of eleven, your eldest child announces that life will henceforth be unsustainable without a computer. The article in question details the health-giving quality imparted to the consumer from 'stress-free food.' Instinctively recognised for centuries, this quality is finally given scientific accreditation. The article says that animals produce stress hormones that are absorbed into the animal's meat and milk and are thereby passed on to humans who eat these products. Our bodies then absorb this second-hand stress in the same way they absorb vitamins and minerals. Stress in animals comes from confinement raising and the feeding of unnatural feedstuffs and stress and diet both create diseases such as diabetes, high blood pressure, obesity, heart disease, depression and cancer.

Your husband has instigated a variety of money-generating projects over the years; sometimes he teaches groups of people a whole range of skills from hurdle making to sheep shearing, and sometimes he spends days at a time building and repairing dry stone walls in a neighbouring parish. One day he injures his back; he is not walling or wrestling with a ram, or performing any heroic feat but merely stretching up to untangle a balloon from a tree. Every year you find more and more of these objects and you are forever watchful and fearful lest the sheep or cattle swallow them. He has a contract to finish a wall by a certain date. You go in his stead.

It seems he does not believe that you have the necessary skill. You have been married for all these years and you realise that you have omitted to tell him that your holidays from the age of thirteen to seventeen had been spent learning to build walls in the Lake District. He is shocked, though not quite as shocked as you are to discover that, even in pain, he is a better cook than you are. Indeed his repertoire of recipes knows no bounds. 'La Cuisine Sans Frontières' as your children call it. You have been itching for a chance to go walling and he has longed to do some cooking. Although you both thought you communicated and discussed everything, this fact had somehow remained concealed.

Suet Puddings

Your husband loves puddings. Every meal he prepares is a mere prelude to the main event and suet puddings feature on the menu at least twice each week; raspberry roll, honey pudding and apple or plum suet. Always the mixture is the same; 8 ounces of your flour with 4 ounces of your suet mixed with a pinch of salt and half a level teaspoon of baking powder and an ample sufficiency of cold water to amalgamate the ingredients. Sometimes suet pastry features as the main course with steak and kidney diced and piled into a suet-lined basin or sometimes it might be a 'swiss roll' shape with bacon and cheese.

The suet roll pastry is mixed with milk instead of water. The rolled out rectangle is spread with 8 ounces of fried, chopped bacon and a small onion, which is then covered with 6 ounces of grated cheese and a sprinkling of parsley. This is rolled up and wrapped loosely in greased foil and then baked in the oven at around 400°F for 45 minutes with a further 15 minutes with the foil opened up to brown the crust.

He often precedes a suet pudding with a light salad; maybe cottage cheese, freshly cooked and still slightly warm beetroot, ripe tomatoes warm from the greenhouse, lettuce, grated carrot, grated apple and mashed potato.

Stew

Sometimes there is a stew with delicious pastry rounds (he refuses to call them dumplings if they do not contain suet) decorating the top. He fries a medium-sized onion in butter and then quickly browns a pound and a half of cubed stewing beef, tossed in flour, in the same butter. This is transferred to a casserole with half a pint of stock and 4 skinned, quartered tomatoes and simmered at 300 degrees Fahrenheit for 3 hours. About 20 minutes before it is ready, the pastry rounds are popped on top, the casserole lid is removed and the temperature increased to 450 degrees. He makes the rounds by rubbing 2.5 ounces of butter into 6 ounces of flour with a pinch of baking powder and a pinch of salt added and mixing with water. He makes this pastry long before he assembles the stew, so that the flour, your own flour, can continue to absorb liquid and be ready to be rolled out later. The 2 inch thick pastry is cut with a pastry cutter; depending on the diameter of the casserole he sometimes needs to let the rounds overlap.

Dough

He also loves experimenting with dough and often makes interesting items by covering dough with chopped apple and grapes and sugar and rolling it up, slicing it and allowing it to rise then brushing it with milk and baking it in a hot oven for quite a short time. He and you and everyone else eat these delectable articles straight away, not withstanding the advice regarding freshly baked bread by which you usually abide. Mrs. Beeton writes a paragraph explaining why it is detrimental to eat hot bread straight from the oven. She insists that it is both unwholesome and indigestible. She suggests that bread should be at least a day old before being eaten. She adds,

"…so firmly was this believed to be the case, that an Act of Parliament was once passed making it illegal to sell bread that was less than 24 hours old."

9.
Food as Medicine

Your Aunt visits you for a week and stays for 22 years. She has just retired early from being an infant school teacher due to poor health. She has limited her diet to a tiny number of components because she gets severe abdominal pain from eating things which, in her words, 'don't digest'. You persuade her to try a few sips of your milk, a substance she previously hated, although, when forced to remember, she admits to having liked it as a child. You explain the difference and tell her, to her amusement and interest, that because she is 'quite old,' the milk she drank as a child is likely to have been safer, fresher and almost definitely unpasteurised. She does not object to being classed as old because she feels old. By the time she dies, she looks much younger and feels healthier than at any previous time in her life. For the first two years after coming to live with you she exists entirely on milk and water. She is so grateful to be free from pain that she cannot face risking eating anything. She loses a considerable amount of weight but feels happy and is quite active and useful.

Eventually she starts to eat again, slowly and carefully beginning with one tiny, wafer thin slice of bread and butter. She loves every mouthful and suffers no ill effects. Over the ensuing days, weeks, months and years, she eats a variety of other things, sometimes with overwhelming pain. Trial and error, suffering and joy gradually help formulate a diet she can tolerate and look forward to. Sadly many substances have to be permanently avoided.

The mainstays of her diet are beef tea, well and slowly cooked porridge, oven cooked pears, bread, butter, milk, of course, and cream, potatoes, stewed Pershore plums and pureed raspberries. Green vegetables continue to cause problems and anything bought-on-a-whim causes near disaster. The digestibility and palatability of everything is a finely judged business. Pears cooked to the proverbial turn are exciting, delicious, energy giving and depression dispersing. Slightly under or over cooked they are the sole cause of all that's wrong in the world.

You try every imaginable way of making porridge. First you make it with water, then with milk and then with a mixture of the two. You all prefer milk but find that the addition of a small amount of water lessens the likelihood of a burnt saucepan. You experiment with oats and oatmeal of varying grades. You begin conventionally enough, pouring medium oatmeal into boiling water in a steady stream from your left hand while stirring constantly with your right. You try soaking the oats overnight, and then next morning, pouring off the liquid and slowly bringing it to the boil before adding the oats. You half cook it and place it in the coolest part of the wood-fired oven for an overnight session. The resulting fare looks more like rice pudding, with its thick skin and lumpy contents, though it is eminently edible. You cook it completely at night in a bain-marie, stirring when you happen to be passing, and reheat it the next morning in the same container; this proves to be the favourite method, by a whisker. You also make porridge with wheatmeal, which is self-sufficiently satisfying, and a great deal more successful than the frumenty you try so often to master, using whole wheat, soaked and cooked forever, usually being gradually brought to boiling point and then transferred to a home-made hay box. The official recipe for this breakfast dish should begin with the words: Preparation time 1.5-3 years. Cooking time at least 24 hours.

Making too large a quantity becomes a common but deliberate mistake. Although it is totally impossible to christen cold porridge imaginatively enough to make it sound appealing, you nonetheless find it delicious, versatile and sustaining. It is eaten with all sorts of fruit, both cooked and raw, honey, nuts, sugar, cream, milk and on its own. Scotland's traditions are highly esteemed in your household, but sadly none of you can bring yourselves to eat porridge with salt.

You, your husband and your children all eat approximately the same components but not always at the same time, in the same quantities or the same combinations. The very gradual and natural way that individual preferences and needs manifest themselves slides into your subconscious. If one of you is below par, the rest of you know instinctively what to give that person in order to begin a restorative process. Your aunt's arrival brings a completely new dimension to life, and every other new person with whom you spend any significant amount of time teaches you all something new.

Some guests almost seem to look after themselves; they are so easy to please on a dietary level. Others, while actively trying to be no trouble, wear you to a ravelling. In your efforts to find food to suit their needs, you only succeed in causing health problems for yourself. The safe common denominators for all, which are the bedrock of why you do what you do, seem to be water, air, milk and bread. The burgeoning wildlife and calm contented livestock are the visible justification.

Food must not only do you good, but also make you feel happy. You say these words over and over again as a mantra. You know they are true and you do not hesitate to repeat them whenever an opportunity presents itself, but it takes years and years before you really understand their true significance. And anyway, they should be said the other way round. You finally realise this. It is only when an individual is happy that any food can do good. Happy in this context means many things; not being under stress, not feeling afraid, not suffering pain, not worrying, not experiencing or conveying anger.

All these things apply to animals too and that is the whole point. Instinctively you have understood and geared your life and your treatment of all creatures, no matter what species, to reflect your beliefs, but only now do all the ramifications hit you. Unhappy people cannot digest food properly, if at all. Unhappy animals do not make beneficial use of the food they are given. You had both experienced many types of farm enterprises over the years and had noticed serious problems being manifested by unhappy creatures trying to eat while under stress.

You chance to meet two animal welfare activists who tell you that they wish they could eat organically but as they travel around the world so much, attending conferences and generally 'dashing about doing good,' they just eat whatever they come across. This strikes you forcibly. After all these years, here, in a nutshell, is the difference between humans and animals. No animal would ever be in such a hurry to do anything that it would neglect its health. No animal would ever want so much to do anything that it would decide to rush somewhere, forgoing good food and then decide to eat something inferior later on. Humans do this all the time and as a consequence their health suffers. It is imperceptible; they are busy and to all intents and purposes happy. Later in life, often too late, they see the choices they didn't know they had at the time.

For years you have observed that if something upsets a persons' equilibrium, whether mentally or physically, that person becomes immediately more acutely aware of, and sensitive, to a whole range of 'vulnerabilities:' slight changes in temperature, over rich food, strong smells, bright lights, human irascibility, knocks and bruises. The weaker or more damaged the person, the greater the adverse effects will be. Taken to the extreme example, when conventional medical experts can find no cause or cure, people are labelled as 'allergic to the twenty-first century.' Milder examples are visible everywhere.

If someone catches a cold, falls over, bangs their funny bone, gets an upset tummy, worries about money or an emotional or romantic attachment, then, straight away, little things which they would not normally have noticed, assume a far greater importance. This is why different people need different food. The more ill someone is, the greater the adverse effect of the wrong food will be and, by implication, choosing the right food will create improvements in both health and temperament.

You invent a liquidised concoction, resembling baby food, which your aunt is reluctant to accept until you start referring to it as soup. This is delicious and sustaining. You experiment with quantities and eventually find a recipe she loves, comprising carrots, beef, potatoes, tomatoes and marrow, when in season. To avoid sameness and repetition you never weigh the ingredients; they do not vary much but each day the emphasis does alter slightly.

Cook and liquidise everything, taking care to remove the tomato and marrow seeds by pressing them through a sieve. You make a small quantity each day to avoid the perils of reheating.

One interesting fact that emerges over the years is that several foodstuffs are only digestible for her if frozen for a while prior to cooking; tomatoes, raspberries, and plums all fall into this category. No doctor can offer an explanation, though many, both retired and currently practicing are asked. All of the older ones tell you that they only received a miniscule amount of instruction about diet during their medical training. As usual, you and she work out your own theory and it holds good, more or less.

During your aunt's sojourn she never once has a day without drinking at least some of your milk. Some days, admittedly, it is only a cupful. To achieve this much-desired continuity of supply though, you end up with more than one cow, in fact more than two cows eventually. An angelic Ayrshire eventually materialises and, although she is a bit surprised to be allowed to rear her own calf, she is nonetheless delighted and gives both it, and you, abundant milk of a supreme quality. It is a juggling game you learn to play and one you believe could never be taught. It is a good game though, for all concerned.

You seriously contemplate renting additional land when some becomes available and you are further tempted when one of your children finds conflicting definitions of 'tenant farmer' in two dictionaries: The Oxford English Reference Dictionary says simply: 'a person who farms rented land' but The Collins Concise Dictionary asserts intriguingly: 'one who rents land from another, the rent usually taking the form of crops or livestock.' You are never going to want to part with livestock, so you try offering the neighbour some produce, accurately anticipating his negative response.

It is a funny thing, you reflect, though finding time to reflect is getting harder, that the wish to be self-sufficient made you work until you could afford a field. Now the need to be self-sufficient and, in particular, the need not to run out of milk, makes you both have to work again to earn money to take on yet more land.

The Politics of Pheasants

When you first bought your field, a few handsome pheasants strolled and strutted about and you delighted in the fact that Christmas dinner could be free from any worries about intensively reared turkeys. In those days there was no organic poultry to be found. You prepare roast pheasant, roast and mashed potatoes, King Edwards of course, sprouts, bread sauce and sloe and apple jelly. You now have dripping in which to roast and fry and lard from the pigs for pastry and for frying delicately flavoured foods. All the discussions about animal fats being less good for you than vegetable oils perplex you. Meat reared on safe, species rich pasture, from animals which have access to trees and hedges will contain a high proportion of essential fatty acids to protect and not harm you. Vegetable oils need to be assessed with regard to how many chemicals they have come into contact with during their cultivation and processing, you feel.

Not that many years later, commercial pheasant shoots start to become popular and lucrative, and the biggest landowner near you constructs huge cages and rears tens of thousands of pheasants. As soon as the shoot becomes a commercial reality, the neighbour makes it clear that he considers that every pheasant, wheresoe'er it roams, belongs to him. He knows exactly how much it costs him to rear each pheasant and he now patrols the area aggressively. Legally, any wild bird on your land belongs to you, but you soon discover just what is entailed in large-scale pheasant rearing and just what the birds are fed on. It is impossible to know which ones are wild and which he has reared.

It transpires that pheasants are reared more intensively even than domestic poultry but as they are technically classified as wild they do not even benefit from the meagre legislation that protects farmed birds. Not only are they overcrowded, but they are also given in their feed a substance which is a known carcinogen and has been banned in the whole of the rest of the European Union. Britain, amazingly and incomprehensibly, asked for and obtained a derogation to continue feeding it to pheasants. This puts you off eating them for life.

One day your husband finds a dead buzzard in your field; it has been shot between the eyes. You are both very upset. Exhaustive attempts to find and prosecute the culprit end in soul-destroying failure. You contact all the right departments and receive assurances and encouragement. The one and only wildlife officer is on holiday but you are bolstered by constant reminders that 'officialdom' is pleased that you have made contact. Two weeks later the officer pays you a visit and tells you that he can do nothing without concrete evidence. He leaves you with a leaflet, in full colour, explaining the feeble nature of the protective legislation. You cannot help wondering what would have happened if a person had been shot instead of a bird. Your have to face the fact that you cannot control everything that happens on or near your land.

You find it easy to think of an alternative Christmas dinner but you can never happily comes to terms with the diminished number of butterflies which coincides with an increase in the pheasant population, nor the visible loss of wild flowers, nor the constant danger posed to all the birds of prey, including the owls. Once they have been released from the rearing pens the pheasants live on your land in large numbers, pecking greedily at seed heads and larvae, not to mention your brassica and raspberries. When the shooting season ends they are left to fend for themselves; it takes a colossal amount of work to exclude them from your vegetable garden.

You read a report about pheasant predation on butterfly populations. No sooner have you read it than you are told it has been superseded by a more recent report commissioned by The Game Conservancy Council, which asserts that no such problem exists. People are forever being bombarded with conflicting information and dishonestly selected statistics. Animals just use their instinct.

In winter, the to-begin-with legal and then, much later in the future, not legal fox hunting takes place just beyond your boundary and in the wider countryside. You find it difficult to choose between the two evils of hunting and shooting.

You do not seek to acquire any further land again until the children complete their leaving home phase, taking with them their very valuable and possibly now indispensable natural resources; they have both become experts in all the skills you and your husband have mastered. You have temporarily forgotten the human flaw of wanting to do things because they are possible rather than vital. What animal, you wonder to yourself, would ever choose to go on a long journey if it was avoidable?

Both children do return eventually, and both are surprised that you are surprised that they both intend to be organically self-sufficient.

10. Water above all Things

After your aunt has been living with you for a number of years you chance to overhear her explaining to your children why she drinks an inordinate amount of water. You all drink water but she is never without a glass in her hand and no one has ever questioned the fact.

Apparently she developed a stone in one of her kidneys when she was in her twenties. She was in constant and severe pain, needing to be taken to hospital regularly, where she was usually given morphine. The stone grew larger and she was told she would have to have the kidney removed. She was, understandably, terrified at the thought, but she could not cope with the pain and there seemed no alternative.

She then received a completely unexpected and initially inexplicable invitation to afternoon tea with the junior partner of her own doctor. It transpired that her case had been discussed and he wanted to offer advice, but knew it would be unethical to talk to her at the surgery. As soon as she arrived at his house, he explained that he too had had a stone in his kidney and he felt she had a chance of avoiding the operation if she followed the regime that had saved him. This was, in theory, a simple process. She would have to drink eight pints of water every day. It was a huge task but his earnestness impressed her and she determined to try.

All the while she was teaching a class of forty-six five-year-olds, except on the occasions when she was rushed to hospital; she could not afford to take time off. She had always been a slim and dainty woman, and drinking vast quantities of water was difficult. At home she was never far from a tap. In school, however, she had to remember to have a large jug of water on her desk. One day, she recounted with a laugh, she forgot to bring a glass. She waited until all the children had gone out at playtime before sipping from the jug. At that moment, a tiny boy popped his head round the door and told her, disapprovingly, that if there was anything worse than drinking out of a bottle, it was drinking out of a jug!

At this point, you walk into the room and sit down to hear the rest of the story, at the conclusion of which you and the siblings are crying, though your aunt is smiling.

She had decided to pay for the operation to be done privately as waiting too long could have been fatal, so preparations went ahead automatically. There was quite a long wait nonetheless but the day eventually came. She drove herself to the hospital, not even thinking it worth mentioning to the surgeon that she had been trying to 'wear the stone away'; she was still in pain and had presumed the regime had not worked.

She was prepared for the operation and was wheeled into the theatre semi-conscious. The surgeon told her that he was going to perform one last cystoscopy to see how the stone was looking. Your aunt was by now feeling so drowsy that she hardly understood what was going on. Then suddenly, the surgeon started dancing round the theatre with amazement and glee.

It was the first time in a long career that he had been able to send a patient home, cured without operating. The huge and knobbly stone, he told her, had started to break up and was passing down the ureter. She remembered then to tell him about her water drinking; he was not only fascinated but genuinely delighted. He absolutely insisted she pay him nothing.

You read that watercress is a valuable source of nutrients and turn your attention to growing some. The stream is undoubtedly clear and perpetual but the cows and sheep have no scruples about where they plant their feet. After some considerable research you eventually identify an ideal position, encourage a tiny breakaway meander, fence it firmly off and introduce some plants. Everyone agrees it was a good days' work.

Deep breathing comes in handy, you find, as a remedy to take anywhere and one which you certainly cannot forget, but water, although slightly less easily transported, can and does seem to cure just about everything. The pain of arthritis recedes miraculously when you only drink water and completely avoid tea or coffee; even your brain and memory work better when drinking a lot of water. Water from different sources contains different minerals and those with discerning taste buds can opt for or even crave water from a particular location. The soil too may be rich, or perhaps deficient, in certain constituents, and a diet derived from a nutritionally unbalanced soil can result in deficiency illnesses.

When you first found your field, you had no idea that any water was deliberately tainted with additives such as fluoride, chlorine or even aluminium. This alarming discovery helps to explain why so many individuals never drink water, as water. The taste of the purest water can and does vary from region to region and there are times when the body requires it to be drunk startlingly cold, and other times when warmed water is comforting. You simply have to ignore the advice you read that all beverages should be neither too hot nor too cold; you all express individual preferences in this respect and the ability to pander to yourselves and change tack occasionally is a fundamental need.

Rainwater, soft water, collected in wooden barrels is the safest, cheapest and most miraculous skin care product. A near neighbour in her nineties has washed her face in it every day of her life, and her face, the only part of her body that is usually visible, peeping out from her long, dull, antique dresses, is as soft and wrinkle-free as a girl of sixteen.

The lichens on your farm indicate the purity of the air. You breath deeply every day, hang out the washing to blow in rain, sun and wind, though never in snow, and always open windows in both the house and greenhouse, no matter how freezing cold the weather, just to give a change of air. Air is free, essential and healing. People and animals react to changes in the weather and they react to wind, perhaps more than any other natural phenomenon. There are days when warm, soft winds lift your spirits and then there are blustery winds which create bad tempers in both man and beast. The sheep seem to be the least affected and can cope with the wind and the cold, but they do not like great heat. The hens enjoy most, the sort of weather which humans like best. Cows appear not to notice, but you notice quite marked changes in their behaviour at milking time if the wind is in the wrong quarter or blowing at too fierce a rate.

Rainwater in barrels has an infinite number of uses. For many years it serves to water plants and to wash just about everything, but always, in the back of your mind, is the prospect of one day making soap. You have the necessary herbs and flowers and you have rainwater. Your husband initiates a policy of keeping the hardwood ash from the open fire separate from the hard/softwood mix in the ash from the wood burner as you are aware that you can only make lye from hardwood ash. You have tallow and lard and soon you will have beeswax.

11.

Bees..Sunshine and Air

In Shakespeare's *Henry V*, the Archbishop of Canterbury talks knowledgeably about bees.

They have a king and officers of sorts,
Where some, like magistrates, correct at home,
Others, like merchants, venture trade abroad,
Others, like soldiers, armed with their stings,
Make boot upon the summer's velvet buds;
Which pillage they with merry march bring home
To the tent-royal of their emperor
Who, busied in his majesty, surveys
The singing masons building roofs of gold.
The civil citizens kneading up the honey.
The poor mechanic porters crowding in
Their heavy burden at his narrow gate…

When reading the play, however, it is important to know that it was written just before it became generally accepted that there was a queen and not a king bee.

These words partly explain your capitulation over using sugar. You simply consider that bees are so clever and live such interesting and organised lives that you feel inadequate, and it is many years before you start beekeeping. One concern is the idea of taking their honey and only giving them sugar in return. This seems neither self-sufficient nor fair. Eventually, you find a beekeeper who coaches you, and who only takes a proportion of the honey, leaving some for the bees too.

Comfrey

You now have honey and beeswax and you can make comfrey ointment, which is supremely useful. Lawrence Hills taught you, not just how and where, but why you must grow comfrey; its supreme virtues as a fertiliser and soil structure improver, as an animal feed supplement and a mender of damaged human tissue, muscle and bones. Soon after the first batch has been made your aunt breaks her wrist and she keeps to her vow of never entering another hospital, but asks you to buy a strong wrist support. She wears this, removing it every two hours to apply comfrey ointment. Three weeks later the wrist is as good as new.

The comfrey plant seems to you to be pure magic; the roots and leaves possess invaluable properties and you continue to learn more about it from books and people for many years. When you tear the leaves into smallish pieces and cover them in a tasteless oil made from sunflower, almond or even your own leaf lard (one of the most useful by-products of pig keeping) and cook this in

the oven with some grated bees wax on a low heat for several hours, the resulting brew is fascinatingly green and mucilaginous. The quantities you use are roughly one pound of lard and 6 ounces of wax with a minimum of 12 ounces of fresh leaves. This needs to be poured immediately into jars before it sets. The leaves can then be used in a hot compress or poultice, but fortunately, in your own long life, you never need one.

You accumulate books containing herbal wisdom and find that the quantities given in recipes vary hugely. All of them seem to work. Some are perhaps stronger, some use elderberry leaves mixed in and others tell you to add glycerine. There are also many books advocating the use of herb oils in preference to ointments or creams. As with cooking and friendships, you fight your way through the multitude of choices.

When you decide to use the roots you first have to choose between two truly conflicting recipes. One tells you categorically to dig the roots in late autumn, after the goodness has been taken back into them from the leaves. The second book tells you to dig the roots in summer. After an appropriate time of agonising you decide to donate the second book to the local village fête; it is perhaps slightly too glossy and contains pretty pictures of many herbs and medicinal plants, but it feels as if it was produced to catch the eye and the captions and advice are sometimes dismissively careless. So you adhere to your old, pictureless text with its genuine and sincere instructions.

In the herb section of the garden, great reverence is accorded to the rosemary bushes. This is because your big, guilty secret has long been that, despite your fascination with alternative therapies and your gradually increasing skill in some areas, you still take painkillers from the chemist when you get a headache. You have great success in curing others by using your own brand of reflexology, which you develop over the years using some aspects of shiatsu, acupressure and zone therapy. Then one day, while rereading a book on culinary herbs, you come across a throwaway line about rosemary oil as a remedy for headaches. You make some and it works. Some years later you try rubbing some on your cheek when you have toothache. That works too. You love this remedy because it is so simple to make.

You gather rosemary flowers (and/or leaves) early in the morning, bruise them slightly in a pestle and mortar with a few drops of organic white wine vinegar (not more than a tablespoonful in total per jar) and then put as many as you can into a honey jar which is already two thirds full of almond oil and shake it thoroughly. You place the jar in a sunny window and shake it vigorously every day for three weeks, after which it is decanted into small bottles of brown glass with screw top lids.

Every friend and family member has his or her own tiny bottle and you get into the habit of making a fresh supply once a year. But sadly it does not work for everyone.

You also make thyme oil in the same way for more serious or migraine headaches and lavender oil for painful muscles and joints. Nature gives you just about everything you need if you know where to look and how to use what you find. You learn to revere honey which you use to clean and heal wounds and you bandage it over stubborn thistles and splinters to draw them out, quite apart from eating it and drinking it with lemon if you have a sore throat (an ailment which you feel you might never have encountered had your children not decided to attend a real school) and occasionally you make candles with the wax. You begin to see a benevolent use for almost every plant: dandelions, chickweed, mallow, daisy, sorrel, watercress, hawthorn, lime and yarrow, but you never ever find a use for betony, other than its aesthetic beauty, despite *Culpepper's Herbal* proclaiming its multiple virtues.

Making Soap

Soap now takes first place in your joint list of priorities. A gradual realisation about how some types of soap, and certainly all the cheap ones are made has been creeping up on you both. Your husband is intent on experimenting. He constructs a stone table-shaped object on top of which he places a wooden barrel containing holes in strategic places. He covers the base of the barrel with washed-clean stones from the stream, followed by layers of hardwood twigs and then a layer of straw. He fills the barrel to within six inches of the top with hardwood ash. He then pours rainwater to completely fill it. A stone vessel is placed to catch the solution that filters through. The whole apparatus is protected from rain, wind and animals: wild, domesticated and human.

The ash solution, or lye, is a mightily dangerous product and he guards it with the care he lavishes on all his many projects. Dedicated equipment is kept for the manufacture of soap and the whole process takes place out in the open air. You make soap with both tallow and lard and varying amounts of beeswax. Sometimes you add honey, occasionally oatmeal. Herbs are used in moderation and experimental colours come from the unlikeliest sources. The happiest problem is deciding whether to make soft soap which you keep in jars, or hard soap which you make by adding a handful of salt and then pour into moulds or trays.

Seriously strong protective clothing, comprising an apron, gloves, face mask and goggles is assiduously worn, and for some years you always embark on this marathon when the children are (relatively) safe at school.

By this time in your lives you are roughly an eighth of the way through your initial delivery of one ton of common salt. This necessary and inexpensive purchase complies with your wish to avoid not only the chemical free-running additives, but also the pollution of seawater by sewage or radioactivity. The first winter of ice and snow necessitated the use of large amounts of salt to keep roads, paths and yards safe to walk in. The salt has now paid for itself and you still have a lifetimes' worth left.

In the dairy the utensils of stainless steel, wood and glass are scrubbed and the muslin and cotton cloths are boiled, but it is the fresh air, wind and sunshine which keep them sweet. You always use a handful of cold wood ash to clean the greasy cooking pans and when you fill buckets with water for the livestock to drink from, you grab a bunch of silverweed to scour them clean before swilling them and, of course, you either tie the handle to a post or remove it entirely to prevent any possibility of a head becoming trapped.

A swarm of bees in May is worth a load of hay is just one of many old sayings you have always known but have hardly ever thought about. Now, as a fledgling beekeeper, you understand, but in line with *'Having your cake and eating it'* you want all the loads of hay too.

Haymaking

Haymaking is wonderful. It is exciting, instinctive, exhausting, risky, therapeutic and worrying. Nothing else matters and every weather forecast, ground-skimming swallow, 'seated' cow, anxious bee and cumulus cloud is watched in minute detail. You are lucky for several successive seasons with hot sun, drying winds, obliging agricultural contractors, adequate grass yields and helping hands, reminding your parents of idyllic childhoods; picnics are de rigeur.

Everyone is ravenous during haymaking and keen to stay in the thick of it, so sustaining, easily digestible, easily-eaten-with-one-hand fare is packed and carried to the workforce. When your father comes to help, tea is brought in an enamel jug, a tradition he will not willingly forgo. Freshly made apple juice suits most of you, often made from last years' good 'keepers': Laxton Superb or Newton Wonder. You each have your own individual container with a hard boiled egg, thinly sliced beef, quartered tomatoes, crisp, sweet, dry lettuce, tiny new potatoes, wholemeal bread and new butter. A fruit sponge made with stewed rhubarb and topped with a cake mixture of 4 ounces of flour, 4 ounces of butter, 4 ounces of sugar, and 2 eggs cooked for 25 minutes at 180 degrees is still alluringly warm, having been taken to the picnic in a hay box.

Then something which may or may not be called global warming, depending on which country you were born in, your political persuasion and the proportion of your income that depends on exploitation, begins to bring about fiercely unpredictable changes in the weather. You are suddenly forced to be grateful that plastic was invented and that silage and haylage exist, just when you had read enough about plastic leaking dangerous substances to want to exclude it completely from your life. There are no more picnics in the hay field but you become adept at moving heaven and earth at short notice.

It soon becomes prohibitively expensive to use contractors. Small farmers are struggling and so it seems are small contractors. Larger contractors increasingly like larger fields with larger gateways for tractors which are huge and can destroy the turf with just a single misjudged turn on a slightly wet day.

Your husband seeks out and attends endless farm sales. Curiously, farm sales only ever seem to take place on very cold days. Lots of people go to them, telling themselves it is too cold to do anything worthwhile at home. Lots of people buy lots of 'bargains' which they cannot resist, and these bargains then rust on their land. Your husband examines very old tractors and their very old engines and bids wisely. He accumulates a tally of three Fordson Major tractors which had been pronounced dead at the scene. Five years later he chuffs and puffs and eventually purrs one round to the front door. It was made so well, he tells you, that it was certainly worth the time he has spent on it and he is confident it will outlive him and he is right.

One very dry year, you use a sprinkler on some vulnerable plants and five adult cuckoos play in the water jets. Later that same year you see a fledgling cuckoo practicing how to fly and take several photographs in the five minutes it takes to perfect the art and fly away. Over the succeeding years you see and hear them less and less often and one day you find yourself comparing cuckoos with hens. You cannot find where you put the porcelain egg you occasionally use to replace a hen's egg in a nest, so you use a very old, misshapen egg instead. The next morning the hen lays a brand new, similarly wrinkled egg. It is not only cuckoos, you think to yourself, that can produce imitations!

You frequently question why you wanted to become self-sufficient. Ideological discussions with your husband usually end when he falls asleep; this is not due to lack of commitment, it is simply tiredness. Everything you do is a joint venture but it seems that, whereas you agonise over every move, he simply gets on and does things.

You imagine yourself in some sort of court, answering detailed and sometimes hostile questions. Are you trying to prove something? Do you envisage being stranded one day in a desert island type scenario? Are you pushing yourself harder than necessary? Is it really important to grow everything you eat? Why not give yourself a rest and buy a few things?

You try to justify everything and yet you question

yourself too. You think how lovely it would be to get some clay from the stream and make some plates in a home-made kiln or maybe to fashion some bowls from a fallen cherry tree trunk. You read avidly about making paper from nettles and long to use the reeds in the pond to make baskets. Why? You cannot answer fully. Do you fear that oil will run out and electricity supplies be severed? Are you overreacting to the takeover of the world by super markets with their dictatorial style and disregard for the natural seasons? If so, you know you are not making much impression. You are not changing the world but they are.

You think while you work, annoyingly you even think while you are reading and you also think while you are glorying in the view and watching the buzzards sliding across the blue above. One day, years late, it hits you. It is all to do with health. You both feel healthy, your children have never had a vaccine or antibiotic and they look the picture of health. It is really the experience of having your aunt living with you which finally helps to distil all the information. Over the years she tells you a bit more about her upbringing; the poverty, the food and, more importantly, the lack of food combined with the intense hard work she did to support her extended family. She had pushed herself to the limit and her body had simply broken down. One doctor tried to insist she have a colostomy but she refused. Mentally she was fine, but physically her body told her to stop eating; she could not cope with the level of pain. But she could not see how she could stop eating, so after a few hours or perhaps a day she would always try again. It was not until she drank your milk that she could see a way to give her digestive system a rest.

Even once she started to eat again, she experienced

many setbacks. If she went out to visit friends and ate something from an unknown source, she always suffered. Gradually she built up a picture, with your help, of not only what she could eat but why.

Over the years she had been to hospital seventeen times and had been examined by general practitioners and high-ranking specialists, but none had ever been able to label her condition, nor cure it. As you and she get older you both meet more and more people, many of whom fortunately are healthy, but many who sadly are not. A number of truths begin to emerge. There seems to be a universal wish for every illness to be given a name, as if that alone would begin a cure. Life, you find, is not that clear cut. All your animals are individuals and so too, it seems, are people. Your aunt's condition has some resemblance to irritable bowel syndrome, some aspects of it led to an early mis-diagnosis of ulcers and, later, to colitis, and all were followed by a doctor-generated regime to which she adhered strictly, which always made her illness worse.

Her eventual decision to abstain from the foods which caused the most pain was also disastrous because it left her, in the end, with almost nothing safe to eat. Meeting fellow sufferers leads to them all realising that they each need their own set of rules and that no blueprint could be suitable for them all. The one vital common denominator is the wish and the physical imperative to avoid chemical residues and additives and to have unfettered access to pure water; of course this does not automatically mean bottled water, about which you have serious misgivings.

She worries initially about eating such a high sugar diet but she feels it is better than not eating at all; the meringues and stewed fruit, and later, much later, little cakes with lemon icing, all play their part in tempting her back to a state where she no longer fears to eat. In fact it seems to provide the spur and give her the confidence to keep trying, as opposed to giving up which, over the years she had so often felt might be the inevitable next step.

Bananas make the occasional appearance in your household and, although they are not home-grown, they are irresistible. You can never forget your English teacher at secondary school telling your class how he blamed everything that was wrong in his life on the fact that he did not have a single banana during the Second World War. Bananas play an important role in your aunt's recovery. She gradually builds up to eating two and sometimes four each day. Great care is taken to buy totally organic ones but once in a blue moon she has a severe reaction and this deters her from trying again for many months. Although these setbacks are rare they are serious. You all feel certain that a chemically treated bunch has mistakenly been sold as organic and you start to make plans to grow bananas. Dismal failure after dismal failure blights this venture until, one day, your aunt discovers Bob Flowerdew on television, describing how he grows bananas in his little corner of England.

Lemons

The most wonderful drink recipe is given to you by a herbalist. He tells you it is simple, delicious and beneficial. Chop and liquidise whole (pips-and-pith-and-rind-and-all) an organic lemon, some organic sugar and pure water in the ratio of 4oz to 1oz to 1 pint adjusted slightly to taste depending on the ripeness of the lemon.

Leave it overnight, then stir, strain and drink it.

While talking to him you remember something you had read many years ago. Long before organic farming was taken even half seriously when, in fact, it was openly derided in the farming press, you noticed a comment warning farmers who liked a slice of lemon in their gin to make sure they bought an organic lemon as the chemicals on the skin of any grown chemically reacted adversely with alcohol.

This was one of many little indicators you had noted. Perhaps the most blatant was one published during bread shortages in the early 1970's. A farmer's wife, writing an article on home bread making, openly advised all farmers wives to ask their husbands to keep a strip of wheat unsprayed and unfertilised for their own use. And then, in 1982, you became aware that the House of Commons catering committee had asked for organic food to be sourced for their kitchens, while ministers were energetically advocating the continued use of agro-chemicals.

A Royal Commission had been established specifically to examine pesticide residues in food. One early morning in December of that year, as you were listening to the Farming Programme on Radio 4, the presenter announced a few of the Commission's findings. These facts were so alarming that the BBC's switch board was inundated with telephone calls from concerned individuals. The Thatcher Government of the day immediately placed a 'D' Order banning the publication of any facts from the report. A trip to the nearest newspaper shop to buy a whole clutch of dailies found a total and ominous written silence.

The radio programme had mentioned that the commission considered that most pesticide residues were to be found on the skins of potatoes and therefore recommended peeling them thickly. Carrots, they concluded, contained worrying amounts in the root, winter-grown lettuce might be sprayed many times with a mercury-based spray and should be avoided and they also recommended that the best way to avoid the chemical residues on wheat was to eat white bread. For some reason, the government felt it was not in the public interest to know this. This last exhortation, which The Commission had evidently intended to be in the public domain, you feel, might well have contributed, or even caused, a seriously large number of health problems. Several years later, the report was made available for purchase from Her Majesty's Stationary Office, 'substantially re-worded.'

It takes a lot of thought and discussion before you both

decide you will buy some lemon trees. You know they will sometimes need heat, so the greenhouse has to be built close to the house in order to be able to use a pipe from the wood burner. The trees are expensive but very exciting to own. Fortunately, your aunt insists on paying for them as she is keen to add one more item to her diet to counterbalance the wonderfully healing but bland and limited choice she has. The benefit you all derive from the lemons soon outweighs the cost.

Not surprisingly lemons trees need to be fed if they are going to produce lemons. After a little bit of trial and error you work out a mixture that suits them and they begin to thrive. The children are fascinated to see trees with flowers, green embryonic lemons and also fully ripe fruit, all at the same time. You feed, or more accurately water them, with lamb droppings soaked in water, comfrey liquid (freshly picked comfrey leaves packed into a barrel and left until a dark brown liquid seeps out of a hole in the bottom, which you then dilute with at least 10 parts of water) and occasionally a few other things for good measure such as wood ash, or water from a variety of sources with different calcium and mineral concentrations.

Lemon Pudding

Lemon pudding is yet another wonderful alternative use for egg yolks. Simply mix together 4 ounces of bread crumbs, 1 ounce of flour, 2 ounces of finely grated suet, 2 ounces of sugar and then add the well beaten yolk of an egg, the juice and finely grated rind of a lemon with sufficient cold milk to form a thoroughly amalgamated mixture, not too wet but definitely not too dry. Put it in a greased basin and steam it for at least 2.5 hours (maybe even 3 according to preference).

Lemon Tart

Possibly the most delicious single pudding ever, also using lemon, is Lemon Tart. Line a 1 inch deep, 6 inch diameter pie dish with pastry, into which you pour a filling made by: creaming together 3 ounces of sugar with 2 egg yolks until the mixture is white. Add the juice and thinly grated rind of a lemon, a gill (a quarter of a pint) of cream, 2 ounces of plain cake crumbs and then fold in the stiffly beaten egg whites. Bake this for about half an hour or until it sets, at 160 degrees.

The children have been brought up without sweets or chocolates and it is your fervent hope that you have done them a favour thereby. You are forever conscious of your own sweet tooth and find it a handicap. This is one of many problems you try to resolve. It is so much easier rearing animals than children. They seem to know what they are supposed to like eating and they just get on with it. You have to make decisions for the children, of course, when they are little and you are constantly under pressure from friends and relatives to let them be more 'normal.' The definition of this word exercised you then, before then and after then, and you die undecided, but remain certain that you are not normal and you are thrilled that you never will be.

Most of your contemporaries at university spent a lot of time trying different diets and so did their parents. The young people were either trying to be extra fit, develop extra muscle, add weight in specific places or remove it elsewhere. The parents were wishing to avoid high blood pressure but, with such a plethora of conflicting advice, almost certainly precipitated its onset: consume two glasses of wine and half a bar of chocolate a day/ never drink alcohol, never eat chocolate but do eat bran/do not eat bran, simply eat the right kind of fat/ avoid fat, drink milk and eat dairy products/avoid dairy products at all costs. It was then that you decided that you wanted to be in control of the production method of all the food you ate.

One day a friend tells you that her child is hyperactive; you think this is a description rather than a label of diagnosis. You learn more. It worries you. Eating nothing but your home produced food and drinking pure water and your milk, the child improves enormously. The improvement is obvious after only three days; the high colour leaves his face and he sleeps better. After a week he is calm and happy and his mother is enormously relieved. There is nothing scientific here. You have heard of exclusion diets but common sense tells you that it is much simpler to make all food safe rather than merely to avoid the worst offenders.

Your friend wonders what she will do when she goes home. You tell her to buy a field; how else can she be sure of any food's history.

This situation, in many different forms, presents itself at intervals throughout the rest of time. An eighteen-year-old with eczema takes three weeks before showing an improvement; she is ecstatic, having arrived one hundred percent sceptical. You suggest to her parents that they buy a field. They smile in agreement. They know you are right but they can do nothing. The industrial revolution has dictated that people must live in towns, divorced not only from the knowledge of food production but also from the psychological, therapeutic and healing power of living on and working on the land.

You are more than a little troubled that so many people

spend so much time and money on cures, yet almost no time or money on prevention. The prevailing ethos, encouraged and fostered by successive governments, concentrates on telling people not to worry when worrying might very well save enormous suffering later.

These reflections remind you of an episode of *'Till Death Us Do Part'*, which you all were glued to when it was repeated one Christmas; your aunt had bought a television by this time. The script writer, Johnny Speight, had given the actress Dandy Nichols a lovely speech setting out her (his) view that the government does not care how many people die from any cause, including easily preventable illnesses, as long as there remains a sufficiently large workforce to carry out essential services. How many people watching would have noticed the points he was making, you wondered. He mentioned the misuse of chemicals in agriculture and the scripts were written some time between 1966 and 1975. John Betjeman's poem *'Harvest Hymn'*, showing that he was fully aware of the consequences of industrial agriculture, was published before 1960. Forty-five years later, one of your children finds an article on the internet giving details of pesticide levels in wheat as if the statistics had only just come to light. Your persistent cynicism is further reinforced when you meet a recently retired high ranking civil servant who tells you that most of his working life has been spent suavely and believably assuring the public there was nothing to worry about when the situation was usually so serious it was actually too late to worry.

For a long time you spend too much energy worrying about the things you are not achieving. You are an idealist who has been forced to lapse. You had wanted to avoid so many things: television, fitted carpets, alcohol, shopping, central heating, banks, drugs, mortgages, insurance, sugar, chocolate, plastic, pasteurised milk, holidays, processed food, genetically modified plants, microwave ovens and cruelty to animals, the latter more than anything, and now that you are in charge of a few you can at least keep them from harm.

You have your own water, milk, wheat, eggs, vegetables and fruit, not to mention compost and various herbal remedies. From the time the children are born until the time they attend secondary school, you are also completely self-sufficient in what will later come to be known as home entertainment. You simply amuse and occupy yourselves and each other. You all play the recorder and playing together is addictively compelling. Three of you play the piano, two play guitars, one masters the mouth organ and you all sing. A debateable number of you are artistic but, most importantly, you all read: Shakespeare, Keats, John Clare, Edward Thomas, Dylan Thomas, Alun Lewis, Stevie Smith, Thoreau, Barbusse, Clare Tomalin, Paul Foot, John Danby, Caroline Spurgeon and dictionaries and anthologies, like The New Penguin Book of Verse in English.

Every year in February, two Canada geese visit you. They swim in the pond and graze in the field and they always leave a few quills lying around which your husband makes into pens. He heats a small tin full of sand in the oven until is very hot all the way through, takes it out of the oven and plunges the feathers in, tip first, and leaves them until the sand is cold. He then takes a very sharp penknife and shapes the nibs to suit individual preferences.

You cut everyone's hair. Having first been invited to cut

your father's hair when you were eleven, a theoretical trauma which he sailed through unscathed, choosing simply to wear a hat at all times for a month, you gradually became an expert. Four people all of the time, five people most of the time and six or more people some of the time has saved quite a lot of money over the years. Your husband is a genius with wood and the house boasts several fine pieces of handmade furniture and of course he repairs anything and everything. But the occupation which, perhaps, gives you all the most satisfaction, is knitting garments from your own wool.

The Joy of Spinning

You are given a spinning wheel on permanent loan and you all try to learn to spin. Your husband perseveres longest and achieves something resembling a ball of wool but in the end it is considered too time consuming. The spinning wheel is returned to its owner to continue not to be used. You find a company willing to spin for you and the hanks of sheep-coloured, unwashed and therefore full of lanolin, wool, possess a waterproof quality. Your aunt is by far the most expert knitter; jackets, coats, socks, hats and gloves all appear in quick succession. Your husband knits rectangles, relentlessly, with very large wooden needles. The result is a soft, lightweight article with loose mesh. You have to take them from him by force before they become too long as soon as you can see a way of turning them to good use. You knit a longer than usual wrap-over cardigan with identical needles and then sew the rectangle onto the welt, skirt-style. It becomes a unique, very warm, light and cosy dressing gown.

A fallen limb of a walnut tree is miraculously transformed into a dozen fabulous buttons and, to complete the sense

of satisfaction you share, each comfortable, exceedingly warm woollen garment, equal to the coldest winter, is given the name of one of the sheep.

Even cracked, sore heals are cured with raw wool. Shoes, boots and slippers are delicately lined and the lanolin effortlessly affects a cure. The same wool can be used for quite a long time and responds well to being gently teased back into a soft, fluffy state.

Allergic reactions to various foods fascinate you and you try hard to prove that it is rarely if ever the food itself but the way it has been grown. It is the same with wool; you are convinced that it is not the wool but any chemicals it may have come into contact with which cause the adverse reaction.

Above all you have health, happiness (which you had

long ago decided really was synonymous with hard physical work), and the land itself, which made you think so often about the 'Eclogue' by William Barnes and in particular the words:

> *"I'd keep myzelf from parish, I'd be bound,*
> *If I could get a little patch o'ground."*

One of your neighbours has a very tall pear tree which is at least a hundred years old. It produces bullet hard, dark green, usually small and sometimes deformed fruit. You ask him what sort of pear it is. He does not know but he says you are welcome to pick as many as you like. Once you have learnt when to pick them, how to store them and how to cook them, you decide they are the greatest fruit on earth.

Forgotten Fruit

Apparently no one in living memory has ever bothered to harvest these pears, partly because of the actual physical difficulty of the task and partly because they look so unappetising. You have to lash your longest extending ladders to the bucket of the fore loader of a borrowed tractor to be able to reach the topmost fruit. The first year you go home at dusk, but your husband stays until it is almost too dark to see and he is determined to reach the very choicest pears which are right at the top of the tree. When he finally comes home he looks pale and shaken but victorious. He explains that, just as he was stretching out into space beyond the top rung of the ladder with an old milk can lined with soft hay dangling from the end of a long handled hoe, hoping to catch the last and best pear by gently jiggling it, the ancient, borrowed tractor rolled backwards half a revolution.

Your husband's heart stopped beating and then made up for it by beating faster than ever before. He showed you the pear.

The pears keep for months. You sometimes peel and poach them whole and sometimes peel, halve, core and cook them slowly and gently in the oven in a covered dish with just sufficient water to cover and sugar or honey to taste. You use eight ounces of raw pears with one ounce of sugar and cover them completely with pure, cold water. They are almost white when peeled. Half way through the cooking process they turn a light orange and then a miraculous pink when they are ready. You all think they are well worth the effort.

12.
'Wild Animals Don't Get Fat'

If you could have lived your life in theory it would have been a very different thing. *'Life gets in the way of living'* was a phrase you said so often to yourself that you could not be sure whether you had actually invented it or whether it was in your sub-conscious. None of you ever gave a moment's thought to your health when you were feeling well but there was no other topic of conversation when anything went awry. You realise more and more clearly as the years pass by, that there are a large number of people who do not know what it feels like to be healthy; not knowing what to strive for, they simply accept how they feel as normal.

For some years everything seems possible and your lovely house has every conceivable feature to make it environmentally friendly, but becoming fully acquainted with your aunt's illness and all the consequences and limitations makes you all reassess your lives.

Before her arrival you had assumed that everyone you knew or met was healthy, unless they told you otherwise. Your aunt's friendly, open, truthful disposition brings forth many previously hidden facts and once people start talking it is soon clear that there is no single solution. There are as many reasons why people become ill as there are people becoming ill. Exposure to toxic substances does not affect everyone the same way and some people thrive on stress while others succumb to it.

It is the same with dieting; there are many different reasons for being overweight and many different types of obesity. There is a bewildering array of diets on offer but in the end people have to work out for themselves a diet that makes them feel healthier and happier. If ever you have an overweight visitor you note with interest that no one ever offers direct advice on losing weight, though everyone advises your aunt on her health problems. It seems as if people feel embarrassed about admitting they have noticed someone's size but they seem sympathetic when noticing that someone is very thin.

You read voraciously about food, diet and the environment and find a reference to the fact that any harmful residues of agro chemicals, which the body cannot excrete immediately, are stored in fat tissue. They can stay there for years, probably doing no harm but, when a person carrying such residues has to cope with a trauma like moving house, getting divorced or deciding to lose weight, the body is suddenly placed under stress and calls on its reserves of energy to see it through the stressful time. But, knowing that a release of emergency energy will also release the chemical residues, the body's mechanism tries to prevent that person losing weight in order to save it from harm.

This only serves to underline what you have always believed; that everyone should eat organically grown food and little or nothing that has been processed. The cost argument against eating organically has always made you close to despair. The true cost of not doing so is never brought in to the equation. Quite apart from the propaganda element, there is also a strong prevailing ethos that it is somehow virtuous to buy the cheapest food. If organic and non-organic food received the same financial support, the cost differential would diminish or disappear altogether.

You also read that food scientists have determined how to manipulate the part of the brain that controls food cravings called the appestat. The appestat constantly monitors the nutrient content of blood and only when fifty-one specific nutrients are present at their proper levels, will an individual feel entirely full and satisfied. Food scientists have found that by adding or subtracting some of these nutrients, they can manipulate a person's sense of hunger and satiety. While the research is still incomplete, it is believed that adding excess fat, sugar and salt to a food tends to make people overeat. Being overweight, therefore, may mean that one is more than likely a victim of this chemical manipulation.

The middle-aged individuals you know who are keen, not to say desperate, to lose weight, almost always eat no breakfast and little or nothing all day, rewarding their abstemiousness with a large meal in the evening. There is something undeniably inevitable about this; working couples need to spend time together and evenings seem the logical time. Your own grandmother had a mantra which she repeated frequently when you were young about eating breakfast like a lord and eating supper like a pauper. You made up your mind to eat frugally in the evenings and heartily in the mornings, ready for the day's work ahead.

No truly wild animal is ever fat, you all agree. Animals whose diet is controlled by humans such as dogs, cats, ponies etc. are frequently overweight. You can think of no examples of creatures, man included, living naturally or in the wild, which are ever fat. Ruminants have to 'work' almost constantly in order to graze or browse a sufficient quantity to sustain their body weight. Hunters are usually lean and have to plan and execute a chase before being able to eat at all.

While your children are studying, one of your guests is dieting and your aunt is slowly gathering strength while doing much of the farm paperwork and washing up, you and your husband enjoy the unremitting outside work. The air you breathe is reason enough for being glad to be alive. You both have a mania for planting trees and you try to find time for collecting acorns and alder seeds, digging up and replanting ash, sycamore and beech seedlings in a safer place and planting willow wands in every available location.

The Orchard

One of the first things you did with your newly discovered field all those years ago, was to plan and plant an orchard. Your grandmother always used to tell you she had been 'born in an orchard' and never tired of reciting the names of the different species and the order in which they became ripe. Plums recalled included Czars, Greengages, Victorias, Pershores, Magnum Bonum, Marjorie Seedling, Bullace and all the damsons. She also reminisced about apple varieties with names such as: Laxton Superb, James Grieve, Newton Wonder, Pitmaston Pineapple and Norfolk Beefing. In addition there were Conference pears, Doyenne du Comice and Williams' Bon Chrétian. She described the excitement she and her siblings felt at going to see if the first plums were ready to eat and then went on to explain how they all helped to pick them. Plums, apples, cherries and pears all had their own unique receptacles for presentation at the wholesale markets. Everything was carefully loaded onto the dray and clip-clopped gently by the pony who could have undertaken the journey faultlessly, without a 'coachman.'

Apples were picked into pots of 40lbs and half pots 20lbs, plums were placed in 12lb chip baskets, as were blackberries too, when abundant, otherwise, like cherries, they were offered in punnets. Many, many times there was such a glut that the price, of perhaps one penny per pound for the choicest fruit signalled the way to bankruptcy. The youngest children in the household of ten always ran first along the lines of fruit trees or bushes and one memory that stayed fresh in your grandmother's mind until the day she died was being allowed to keep the 'tuppence' she was given for a punnet of especially large raspberries.

One problem you have to solve very early on in your chosen life concerns straw: how much to buy and when to buy it. Although you manage to be self-sufficient in wheat, the small acreage you grow yields only a tiny amount of straw. If you buy some 'off the combine,'

thus saving the farmer the expense of carting, stacking and reloading, it is far cheaper. The downside is that you have to pay for it sooner and find somewhere to store it. The first few years you buy bales as and when you need them, but once you have calculated the cost it becomes apparent that you must buy at the most opportune moment and in reasonable quantities to keep down the cost. You must then, in addition, buy a plastic sheet to protect them as you have no spare space to store them in the barn.

Another decision bordering on a problem concerns the bull. You need your cow to have calves in order to produce milk but you cannot possibly justify or afford to buy a bull. you then either have to hire (or borrow) one or to use artifical insemination. There are arguments for and against both options but you do not have the luxury of choosing. In the beginning the cow you buy is already in calf. The next time a neighbour offers to lend you his bull. On a subsequent occasion you do use artificial insemination but you both wish you owned your own bull.

Your aunt's health comprises more layers of complexity than any of you had thought possible; she feels it is simply because she has been suffering for so long. She was never offered any medical advice that helped and so she soldiered on, eating less and less until her body came to a halt. At least she is happy. She has the mental and physical safety net of knowing she can stick to milk if the pain is overwhelming, but she does want to get better.

She has had many brushes with different branches of the medical profession but more often than not she has been made to feel that her illness is psychosomatic. One day, by a happy chance, a retired doctor offers her an explanation which seems wholly feasible. He feels that the action she has taken to avoid too much pain by cutting down the number of substances she eats has, in itself, exacerbated the problem. He tells her that she cannot live forever without eating. She had suspected this. He goes on to explain that her digestive system has now forgotten how to deal with large numbers of foods. This is why, whenever she tries something new, the pain is too severe and she associates that particular pain with the food. In fact, he continues, she must keep trying new things, but only in miniscule quantities in order to re-educate her system. Then, eventually, her digestive juices will not be thrown into such turmoil by any new substance and slowly her system will learn to choose the right ones to digest what is being eaten. This is delightfully unscientific but he stresses that since retiring he has dispensed with technical, diplomatically careful, medical language and is practicing being a human being. This all makes perfect sense to your aunt.

She willingly tries new things, in homeopathically minute quantities. It is perhaps your solid, golden, meringues which trigger an improvement. She loves them. They make her look forward to what is otherwise a series of tiny, bland meals; she can never yield to an impulse of biting into a raw apple, carrot or plum without paying too high a price. Another step forward is the realisation that she cannot tolerate the seeds in cooked raspberries. You and she know that you should have admitted this fact sooner; both tomato and marrow seeds had always been carefully avoided. The raspberries, slowly stewed after a few months in a deep freeze, had been such a delicious boon, and they looked so harmless that she had been extremely reluctant to swap their visual beauty for a dish of purée.

Slowly, new facts come to light about her diet both as a child and a young adult. Ignorance and poverty had colluded to provide a truly atrocious diet. She had lived with her parents and her younger brother in a damp, unheated house and her mother had always bought the cheapest food. They produced milk and butter, cream and eggs, wheat, oats and barley but most of this was sold, and the quality of the food they ate was given the lowest possible priority. Overripe, imperfect and therefore unsaleable fruit was abundant in the autumn, but for much of the year there was little choice. Very fat bacon, laboriously salted and hung in the rafters of an intermittently smoky kitchen was a staple food. White bread with the most awful, hard-bordering-on-rancid butter with tinned jam, allegedly and probably made from swedes flavoured with raspberry. Even though they kept hens, most of the eggs were sold and the children were given half an egg twice a week if they were lucky. They also had some ghastly, waxy cheese.

When your aunt first felt inclined to try your bread you made special loaves with thrice-sieved flour. She had felt an instinctive fear of bran. She loved the bread. You both knew that she needed all the component parts of wholemeal flour but in the end it took several years of incremental bran inclusion, a quarter of an ounce per baking, before she was eating a hundred percent real flour.

One of the many doctors she had seen over the years had been aggressively certain that there was no such thing as stress. One was either ill, or not! He required that you have something identifiable and convenient, which he could look up in a textbook; anything else had to be your imagination. She knew he was wrong. Yet he was adamant and he also believed unyieldingly that it was not possible to catch a chill. If you sat in a draft and developed a stiff neck, he would assert that you had injured your neck without realising. Equally, he refused to acknowledge the existence of a chill in the stomach, which you and your aunt had definitely suffered on numerous occasions. No wonder his wife had left him, you thought to yourself.

13.
The Next Generation

If nothing else your life had been an erratic accumulation of disjointed pieces of evidence and information, most of them proving to you beyond doubt that humans are far too slow to learn and that they almost never take advice or learn from each other's mistakes. In this respect they are totally unlike all the other animals you have ever known.

At the age of sixty-one, your husband is healthy, happy, busy, useful, beloved and dead. You do not and cannot speak; your vocal chords are paralysed. Just hours after his body is taken out of the house, the bees come in to inspect the room where he died. They come in and out, quietly and knowingly for several weeks and then they leave. Death is an all or nothing affair, rather like farming. You have much time to reflect on the fact that *"This little world shall so wear out to nought"* as Shakespeare warns us all in King Lear. When you were young you felt certain that your useful contribution to saving the planet lay in loving and caring for a *'little patch o' ground.'* You have always followed world events closely and you are not happy with what you see. So you concentrate hard on the little world around you.

A lifetime's experience has taught you to be a fair judge of the many types of utterances of which an average cow is capable; these range from crooning and mooing to roaring and a high pitched trumpeting. The wildlife on your farm, however, still emits a range of sounds which manage to both shock and fascinate you. Grass in summer is especially noisy. The crickets and grasshoppers are obvious candidates for singing awards but there are many more tiny sounds, all the more noticeable on the stillest of hot days. It is important to sit so that you are on the same level as the flowers. Everything visual assaults you first, but gradually the music comes through the waving seed heads and imagination begins to play its part. After all, you have recently read that grass screams when it is cut so perhaps it also hums happily to itself when left alone. The louder sounds of wind through the trees or Keats' rustling, withered sedge, fast flowing streams and miniature waterfalls all re-enforce the superfluous nature of any music chosen to accompany wildlife films on television.

Every year, as the foxes and deer take it in turns to scream make-believe murder from the wood, you find yourself wondering if perhaps some ritual atrocity is, after all, being enacted there. Their repertoire of sound is extensive and you feel that the intimate lullabies to which they treat their newborn might just qualify as song.

Some of your visitors mistake the black-winged music of the rooks and jackdaws hang-gliding low over the barn roof on their way to bed, for ominous portends akin to Hitchcock's thriller 'The Birds'. Yet birds sing from sheer happiness, on cool November days or on balmy August evenings with all nesting done. The fairy notes of the goldcrest in the wood last deep into the winter; perhaps this is the point where definition is paramount. Perhaps your birds are not singing but merely calling. It is all music to you.

You value the darkness on and around your isolated-by-hills farm and feel an affinity with those who talk nostalgically of the dark skies of their youth. The darkest night is light enough to find your way. You also treasure the lack of sound pollution. All the wild creatures and, for that matter, all the domesticated ones too, can sing, call and communicate without competition.

Though what seems at first to be silence, when penetrated deeper, is layers of delicious sounds, whispering and shushing along invisible wave lengths: the sudden loud, hurrying wings of a heavy pigeon fighting clear of the Philadelphus buds and struggling uphill until it has just enough air to free-fall in, the now almost forgotten music of the thrush banging a snail on a stone, the memory of the skylark hanging crotchets and minims in the air, or the newly fledged greenfinch so unmusically singing for his supper.

A group of university students knock on your door one day and ask if they can carry out a bird survey. They explain in more detail what they wish to do; they want permission to come and go at irregular but frequent intervals during the coming year, armed with binoculars and notebooks. You readily agree and they proceed to merge into the landscape and your sightings of them are as rare as theirs of your secret barn owls. At the end of the year they present you with a long list of species, several highly coloured maps and a couple of graphs showing national bird distribution.

You have tried to live and farm, causing the least possible disturbance to all the creatures which share your land. These young people fully intend to spend their working lives erecting nesting boxes and then raiding them, albeit gently, weighing newly hatched chicks, tagging, tracking and 'drawing conclusions' which they will then publish. You are deeply unsettled by these revelations. A long discussion follows but they can no more allay your fears than you can dent their absolute conviction that they will be helping to save the lives of many birds. Never have you made less impact, never felt more helpless. You think of little else for weeks and finally try to lessen the depression by writing.

> *"The Blackcap Warbler weighs three quarters of an ounce",*
> *No-one has the right to know that.*
> *They belong to nobody but themselves*
> *Let's leave the birds alone.*

> *"Until recently (1964) it was thought that*
> *Chiffchaffs could always be told from*
> *Willow Warblers by their darker legs, but*
> *Intensive trappings have shown that some*
> *Willow Warblers also have dark legs."*
> *They know what they're doing and*
> *What colour their legs are,*
> *Let's leave the birds alone.*

The Next Generation

"The spots on the tongue-spurs of a young Hedge Sparrow are black
Those of the Willow Warbler are brown
Whereas the Garden Warbler has pale purple spots on
either side of the base of the tongue,
And the Chiffchaff has none".

You trespass whoever approaches to see,
Let's leave the birds alone.

You read about a newly formed committee, charged
with deciding when a non-food can be called a food.
This too sounds alarming. Products, genetically
engineered by man and fashioned to look like familiar
foods by man, are now being sold as food, all because
of a man-made decision. If, in the view of the members
of the Committee for Novel Foods and Processes, the
engineered substance is 'substantially equivalent' to the
naturally evolved model on which its shape and taste are
based, it can be licensed as a food. This seems to you
like evolution on 'fast (food) forward' and with potentially
dire consequences. It's like taking someone's child and
giving a substantially equivalent one in its place. The
child may be the same age, be the same height, have
the same hobbies, the same colour eyes and hair but,
almost as an afterthought, the instigator might say:

"Oh! her handwriting's different,
And of course she won't love you
But that is a small price to pay.
You can comfort yourself
You're a servant of Science
Something not many can say."

On an every day level the number of friends and relations
who are either ill or dying or worse saddens you. You
have given and been asked for advice so often but now
you are old, and you meet, by chance, two young people

135

who teach you. They come from opposite ends of the country but their stories run parallel and, although they never meet, you see them and hear from them both almost simultaneously. The young woman has suffered a severe reaction to a solvent while helping to renovate a house. It is a massive problem and requires a radical, if not desperate, remedy. Her liver is damaged and she has no energy; many everyday substances with which she comes into contact now cause further deterioration in her condition.

Part of the desperate remedy involves divorcing herself from each and every person who has, at any time, visited this house; the solvent lingers in people and objects and even in minute quantities it has the power to make her very ill. You listen to long and detailed accounts of this young woman's search for a diagnosis and then a cure and you cannot help thinking about all those individuals who might suffer similarly, but lack her medical knowledge and tenacity to obtain an explanation for the symptoms she is suffering.

The second new friend has refused all conventional cancer therapy and has embarked on a lonely voyage to discover how to heal himself. This young man's search for the right path to take leads him to study the healthy people on this planet. He reads about remote tribes who have never experienced certain diseases and he finds out about their diet. It is a slow and painful process and although he feels ill and weak he will not give in.

By independent and unique routes, these two people arrive at very similar conclusions. They both contact you in their search for pure milk. You happen to have some to spare. Your extended family requires more than one cow and there are plenty of volunteers to do the milking.

The young man believes he has to consume an entirely raw diet, heavily dependent on organic milk, butter and soft cheese, made regularly. Raw eggs too play a very important role; he swallows sixty each week. He eats raw chicken, fish and beef and industrial quantities of vegetable juices, made freshly each day from celery, carrot and beetroot.

It is all very well if you are in good health but it is not so easy if you are feeling ill. This extreme diet is, in every way, hard to take. For months there is never a day when he does not feel sick, and despondent. Gradually you learn details about his initial time in hospital. He was admitted for tests which he hoped would identify the root causes of the severe fatigue he was plagued with but no diagnosis offered any real help, and he was 'guinea-pigged' into course after course of injections. He felt strongly that these drugs caused the cancer and the chemotherapy he was subsequently offered felt more like a death knell than a cure.

There are so many things that these two people have in common, yet neither seems to need the other; they have both walked their lonely paths and found their own particular solutions. The young woman's sensitivity to everything has been heightened. She knows within seconds if she is in a safe environment. Her whole being reacts to everything she can smell, see, hear, touch, eat or drink. Her body knows, without any need of documentation, if the food she is eating is really making her better. The milk and meat from genuinely happy, relaxed and secure animals, eating absolutely pure pasture and drinking absolutely pure water, transform her. If she is ever given food from caged, stressed or non-organically fed animals, her body knows immediately, even if she tries to tell her brain to override these feelings. She feels strengthened by your milk, eggs and meat. Unlike him, she never eats chicken but they both eat fish. She eats cheese from time to time but does not feel the same imperative need for it. The young man eats minimal amounts of fruit and never touches apples although he does eat oranges. She only eats very hard, unripe apples but she also eats cherries, mulberries, raspberries and bananas. They both agree that vegetables supply more reliable and lasting energy.

Potatoes have always been a major food item for you and your family but they play no part in these young peoples' diets. A friend you met thirty years ago, with acute allergic reactions to almost everything, lived for at least ten years on potatoes, morning, noon and night. More difficult for either of them to explain to you is the fact that, whereas he can eat several root vegetables, she eats only those which grow above ground. Neither of them would go within a mile of processed food of any description nor within two miles of sugar or salt. They both react violently to influences which healthy people fail even to notice: power lines, solvents, exhaust fumes, fluoride, chlorine, agricultural chemicals, and household detergents, to name but a few. Both young people cherish an ambition to find a field and be self-sufficient.

At about this time you receive a communication by post from a man who lives in Plymouth. You cannot describe it as a letter; it is more of a note, written with a fountain pen, in hard-to-decipher-handwriting. He squashes his few words on the clean white top of an old printed advertisement leaflet. 'More power to your elbow' he scrawls. He says he wishes he had bought a field and a cow many years before. He developed Multiple Sclerosis, which was not diagnosed correctly for several years. His wife left him because she could not understand his behaviour. After a huge effort, researching relentlessly with rapidly deteriorating eyesight and confined to a wheelchair, he concluded that he needed raw organic milk with its myelin content, and eventually he managed to secure a supply. Drinking one pint a day effected a marked improvement. He wrote simply to tell you. He gave no address.

You are especially interested that one of your new young friends has discovered research suggesting that washing up liquid adversely affects genes and chromosomes. You have always recoiled from it; not psychologically but physically. Your hands react and within a minute or less, your whole body feels uneasy and damaged.

When you meet them, both young people are lacking in energy and stamina. Within eighteen months both display a marked improvement. It is an ongoing battle; they are constantly alert to the dangers of loosening their military regime. It saddens you and uplifts you by turns. You want to share their experiences with others you meet later, but, in line with everything life has taught you, no one wants to be told; they all want to find out for themselves and, of course, as regards personal health, that is how it has to be. The infinite variations in human make up demand infinite, finely tuned solutions.

Before your children decided to have children of their own, they questioned you about your diet when a child. They asked about your mother's diet and her mother's. It transpired that they had heard a radio programme which presented a compelling argument linking a child's health and intelligence to various factors not only at and after conception but also before it. They wanted to know if you had ever smoked or imbibed alcohol and whether your diet leading up to and during pregnancy was nutritionally balanced. They actually admitted that the programme was so convincing that the only obvious conclusion was that no one should ever have any more children. This fatalistic, though not entirely pessimistic attitude, lasted for several years.

In no respect could you guarantee either purity of diet or lack of vice back into pre history but you did tentatively point out that as they were glowing examples of fit and healthy humans with good academic ability into the bargain, the risks might not be too high. Grandchildren and great-grandchildren appear at intervals thereafter and you continue to note contentedly, the zeal with which both of your children maintain control of their home-grown food supplies.

At 97 you are, in your own words, beginning to feel your age. You take pleasure in watching the younger generations mastering the skills you devoted your life to achieving. You relax in your armchair, feeling secure in the knowledge that your little piece of land will continue to provide for your descendants, and that they share your philosophy, when you chance to overhear one such fourteen-year-old talking to his mother: "Mum, do I have to eat organic, wholemeal bread? None of my friends has to eat it. Come to think of it, none of my enemies has to either."

The End.

By the same author

The Secret Life of Cows
By Rosamund Young

Cows can love, play games, bond and form strong, life-long friend-ships. They can sulk, hold grudges, they hvae preferences and can be vain.

All these characteristics and more have been observed, document-ed, interpreted and retold by Rosamund based on her experiences looking after the family farm's herd on Kite's Nest Farm in Worces-tershire.

Here the cows, sheep, hens and pigs all roam free. There is no forced weaning, no separation of young from siblings or mother. They seek and are given help when they request it and supplement their own diets by browsing nibbling leaves, shoots, flowers and herbs.

Rosamund provides a fascinating insight into a secret world - secret because many modern farming practices leave no room for displays of natural behaviour.

The Secret Life of Cows is not only a study of family and herd re-lationships, communication, grieving and playing but makes for a highly readable and poignant study littered with anecdotes that will make the reader laugh, wonder and reflect. Certainly it will make you look at the domestic cow in a different light.

The Secret Life of Cows Published by Farming Books and Videos (now The Good Life Press) ISBN 1904871119

Reviews of
The Secret Life of Cows

No scientific study of cow psychology could equal Rosamund's account...She has made the term 'animal sentience' come truly alive. We can only be thankful that she has.
Joyce D'Silva, Farm Animal Voice

'The Secret Life of Cows' provides scientific evidence (for science is fundamentally about observation) by working farmers, not just of the sentient nature of farm livestock, but their individual characters, intelligence, capacity for learning and recognition of their keepers.
Robin Maynard, The Ecologist

Without hesitation I would name Rosamund Young's book as my book of the year. Rosamund, whose family are pioneers of the organic movement, has written a little masterpiece of animal sentience, that she would prefer to call bovine friendships. What is entrancing, apart from her gift in being able to enter the lives of animals, is the way it speaks directly from the heart, with such simplicity and no sentimentality, humorous and serious at the same time. For all its passion, concern and love, what comes across too is her hardheadedness. This beautifully illustrated book is both a rhapsody and a practical handbook. I have not read anything remotely like it.
Philip Callow, The Oldie Magazine

'The farmer who rents our fields for his bullocks recently noticed he had one extra, small, black and furry-eared. It turned out he had decided to leave his solitary life miles away to cross a busy dual-carriageway and join our herd. Our farmer bought him and here he stays. So nothing surprises me about cattle. Mrs Young at Kite's Nest Farm has been watching their behaviour since 1953. She and her parents before her have treated each animal as a named individual. Each, she says, are as varied as people: bright or dull, friendly or aggressive, proud or shy. Cows have good memories and learn from experience. They play games and make best friends. As a result, she feels passionately that farmers have 'a moral obligation' to treat their animals humanely. This is an inspiring book and, I think, important.
Leslie Geddes-Brown. Country Life

'The Secret Life of Cows' made me laugh out loud and moved me to tears. It should be required reading for every veterinary student, agricultural student and farmer in the world!
Tricia Holford, The Born Free Foundation

The scariest book I read this year was Rosamund Young's 'Living with Cows' (sic) which applies Jane Goodall's approach to chimpanzees to a species on the verge of extinction in Britain, the freerange domestic cow. The characters in Young's herd—kind, ingenious, affectionate, as strongly marked as you or me by individual likes and dislikes — make a travesty of the sickly, short-lived, mechanised beasts we have bred to replace them. I hope this book helps reverse the trend.
Hilary Spurling, The Daily Telegraph

This really is a riveting and unique insight into understanding the nature and behaviour of the cow. Rosamund Young recounts her experiences of working with her family farm's herd in Worcestershire and the results of having cows, hens, sheep and pigs that all roam free. Arguing for compassion in farming and an adherence to a more organic, sustainable coexistence with animals, this book offers an entirely alternative perspective on how we interact with livestock.
Permaculture Magazine.

The following is an extract found on Alan Bennett's blog

24 August I am reading The Secret Life of Cows by Rosamund Young. a delightful book though insofar as it reveals that cows (and sheep and even hens) have far more awareness and know-how than they are given credit for it could also be thought deeply depressing. Though not if you're a cow on Young's farm, Kites' Nest in Worcestershire, which has been organic since before organics started and where the farm hands can tell from the taste alone which cow the milk comes from. Young makes the case against factory farming more simply and compellingly than anyone I've read and simply on grounds of common sense...it's a book that alters the way one looks at the world and one which all farmers would do well to read.

The Good Life Press
P O Box 536
Preston
PR2 9ZY
01772 652693

The Good Life Press publishes a wide range of titles for the smallholder, farmer and country dweller as well as Home Farmer, the monthly magazine aimed at anyone who wants to grab a slice of the good life - whether they live in the country or the city.

Other Titles of interest

A Guide to Traditional Pig Keeping by Carol Harris
An Introduction to Keeping Cattle by Peter King
An Introduction to Keeping Sheep by J Upton/D Soden
Build It! by Joe Jacobs
Cider Making by Andrew Lea
Flowerpot Farming by Jayne Neville
Grow and Cook by Brian Tucker
How to Butcher Livestock and Game by Paul Peacock
Making Jams and Preserves by Diana Sutton
Precycle! by Paul Peacock
Showing Sheep by Sue Kendrick
Talking Sheepdogs by Derek Scrimgeour
The Bread and Butter Book by Diana Sutton
The Cheese Making Book By Paul Peacock
The Pocket Guide to Wild Food by Paul Peacock
The Polytunnel Companion by Jayne Neville
The Sausage Book by Paul Peacock
The Secret Life of Cows by Rosamund Young
The Shepherd's Companion by Jane Upton
The Smoking and Curing Book by Paul Peacock
The Urban Farmer's Handbook by Paul Peacock

www.goodlifepress.co.uk
www.homefarmer.co.uk